My Inner GPS

A Road Map to Manifesting a Meaningful Life

Infinite Intelligence
Mathilde Benmoha Carro

B'H

My Inner GPS
A Road Map to Manifesting a Meaningful Life

ISBN 978-1-73230-931-9
Printed in Canada

Library of Congress Control Number: 2019903769

Y & Y Publishing
Quebec, Canada
yandypublishing@gmail.com

Ordering Information:
Special discounts are available on quantity purchases by corporations, associations, educators, and others. For details, contact the publisher at the above-listed email address.

Acknowledgements

To the Creator- The 'One' and Only Source
of Everything

To Joshua with Love
Thank You

"You are wherever your
thoughts are, make sure your
thoughts are where you want to be."

-Nachman of Breslev

Table of Contents

"Everything is energy and that is all there is to it. Match the frequency of the reality that you want and you cannot help but get that reality. It can be no other way. This is not philosophy. This is physics."

-Albert Einstein

Preface

This book is the result of years of soul-searching. It is the brainchild of wanting to be more. There may come a time in our life when we realize that the reality we see and know is not all there is. This leads us to question everything- our purpose, our existence, and our essence- the consequence of which is a desire to understand reality beyond its appearances. The moment this shift occurs, that is when we are ready to delve into the metaphysical in search for answers and understanding. We all heard the expressions: 'mind over matter', 'our thoughts create our reality', or, 'positive mind for a positive life', etc... However, on a practical level and in our daily life how does that really work? If it were that simple to create a desired reality, then there would be no suffering, disease, poverty, hunger, etc... Everyone would be happy, blissful, healthy, and prosperous. Therefore, there must be more to this theory than it appears on the surface.

My research has brought me to learn the works of many extraordinary people that I today consider mentors. I encourage anyone that is looking to expand their knowledge on the subjects of mind science, metaphysics, positivity and personal development to read the works of James Allen, Shalom Arush, Genevieve Behrend, Henry Harrison Brown, Ernest Holmes, Chaim Kramer, Bob Proctor, Judge Thomas Troward, Napoleaon Hill, Menachem Mendel Schneersohn, Viktor Frankl, Claude Bristol, Wallace Wattles, David J. Schwartz, Joseph Murphy, Wayne Dyer, Nachman of Breslev, Sadhguru Jaggi Vasudev, Louise Hay, Jim Rohn, Earl Knightingale, Catherine Ponder, Stuart Wilde, Florence Scovel Shinn, the Bible and the Psalms to name a few.

The common denominator that stands out when we read the works of these great authors is their genuine desire to help everyone transform their reality and negative conditions. These exceptional beings all share the same lifeward goals: promoting positive expansion, kindness and our Divine right to live a meaningful and abundant life. I am writing this book with a similar wish and to convey a comparable message, but in my own unique way and based on my own experiences and understanding.

There is a sea of authors, experts, books, workshops, videos, lectures, and seminars that cover these life-changing concepts. Many are available in the public domain and are easily accessible to all. There is no reason or valid excuse why anyone cannot do this. One must only *desire* and *want* the knowledge. Once we start our journey of growth and transformation, we do not want to stop. These theories and concepts, with all that they encompass, expose us to new ways of seeing and thinking; it touches our inner being. Our thirst for truth will no longer tolerate the *status quo*; it will ignite in us the momentum to push onward, to evolve, and to change. Do not resist this change; be open and receptive, follow intuition; it will not deceive you. What we learn makes us better, stronger, and connected to the Source of everything. In an attempt to assist the reader to understand some of the complex concepts and ideas in the book, certain ideas and concepts are repeated several times, in various places throughout the book- all with the intent to ensure that the reader grasps them well and thus, can apply them with ease. This book will definitely help anyone in his or her quest for a better reality. It will clarify the ideas, steps, and techniques for manifesting a meaningful life.

"What you think; you become. What you feel; you attract. What you imagine; you create."

-Buddha

Introduction

A few years ago I started looking for existential answers and understanding. I was not where I wanted to be. In my mind, I was not clear on my life's goal and purpose. I was confused and searching for answers. On the surface, you can look and portray the image of the most happy and accomplished person. However, on the inside, there was something missing. There was a feeling of emptiness and longing for something more; it was not something easily comprehensible to me. I started researching and reading on the subjects of mind science, metaphysics, and self-betterment.

What I learned early on was that I was not alone, and furthermore, that the path to significant transformation most often comes from a place of pain and a deep need for self-improvement. I learned that suffering in any form has one amazing quality- to bring out the hidden potential in every one of us. We are all born with an inner genius and are able to do or be anything we wish to be. However, the paradox lies in the fact that most of us will not tap into that inner treasure because we are living a seemingly comfortable life. I wanted to understand more about that 'inner treasure' we all possess and almost never use. My quest for answers has taught me so much and led me to make significant changes in my life. I had to change the way I think, speak, and act. I discovered my 'inner GPS', my personal Global Positioning System, which is none other than my inner 'G_d, Power, Solution'- that amazing treasure we all possess. We are all meant to live happy, healthy, and prosperous lives- that is the 'Eternal Truth' of life. However, over time, this Truth was lost or forgotten. We started to find different reasons (such as circumstances or conditions) to understand reality. This Truth became a long lost concept that we seldom think of, or believe and apply.

The life we have, i.e., our reality, is a reflection of our inner thoughts and feelings. The basis of mind science is that our mind, (conscious / subconscious), through our thoughts, shapes our reality. Our beliefs and the thoughts we focus on most are at the root of our reality. If our main thoughts are not aligned with the Eternal Truth, then we will not manifest what we want. I must confess that, at first I was a little resistant to this idea. I refused to believe that we attract to ourselves our reality by just thinking. How was that logical? How can you tell someone that is sick that they are responsible for their sickness- that it is their own doing? I thought to myself, 'this cannot be true'; no one wants to be unhappy, negative, down, sick, poor, angry, resentful', etc... I essentially learned that, yes, it is not only possible, but it is so. There is a whole science behind this theory and whether we are aware of it or not, we are in fact manifesting our desired or undesired realities.

The decision to write this book was fueled by a desire to share all of these life-changing findings. The road to a better me was not simple (and it is ongoing). At first, it was full of obstacles and challenges. Any new beginning can seem overwhelming, but once we start, we wish we had started long ago. As we grow and understand the deeper meaning of being, we gradually let go of doubts, anxieties and fears. We all have something we fear or want to change or improve. To grow and evolve is a natural aspect of life. We are not meant to stay static or to resist change. We are created to develop and mature. As such, it is natural to want to expand our horizons (to aspire to be better). It means to live according to the Divine plan. A lasting transformation can only come with will and sincere desire. We are each unique and have an individual purpose to accomplish in this physical world. We need to be open-minded and to resist conformity. We need to ponder on the idea of 'who we truly are', or, 'Why do we exist?' We are all made of a 'physical self' and a 'spiritual self'. In essence, what we need to comprehend is that we are not only a body with a mind, but we also have a soul. Our life force is our soul, without it we are simply a lifeless mass. The Creator made us this way, with a body, mind, and 'soul' so we can be connected to Him (the Source of everything). We are all part of G_d, the Creator- and we are all one. To truly grasp, and not just accept the depth of this concept, inspires us to be more and therefore, to become the amazing human beings we were meant to be.

When we understand that we are not 'a human body experiencing spirituality', but rather, 'a soul experiencing a human body', then we can start to make sense of man's eternal struggle between ego and spirit. Our higher purpose is for our ego (physical self) to serve our spiritual self. However, in practice the opposite occurs, our spirituality supplements our ego. When this multi-layered idea, of body, mind, and spirit is understood, our life's journey takes on a different meaning. In daily life, this means, we must try to include the Creator / Source Energy / Infinite Intelligence in our thoughts, words, and actions. We should not make material pursuits our primary goal (the idea is to prioritize), but instead we need to give spirituality a central place in our life. However, most of us are not there yet.

Mind science is the science of 'mind power'. We are able to create anything through the use of our mind. However, in practice, we are not aware of how powerful our mind is. We are not using this powerful tool the Creator gifted us. We hardly give any thought to the way we can use our mind. We can use our mind to create either a positive reality or a negative one. When we use the mind the right way, the intended way, we can do anything we want and manifest a positive reality. In the same vein, when we use it in the negative way, the unintended way, it can create havoc and chaos in our lives.

To know and apply mind science means to become aware of our thoughts and beliefs and to see how they affect our ability to manifest our desires, or, to realize how they are actually stopping us from having the reality we desire.

As such, it is indispensable for us to find out why we are thinking, speaking, and acting as we do, so we can change what we do not like. Mind science explains the process to follow in order to manifest a positive reality. I like to think of mind science as the science of positivity. The more positive our thoughts are the more positive our reality is going to be. Positive beings vibrate at high frequencies and send out into the Universe the right energy to attract the reality they want. We are like boomerangs, the thoughts and energy that we transmit into the Universe will come back to us in like energy. In practice, to experience a desired reality we need to be aware of our thoughts and feelings, and we need to make sure that they are overwhelmingly positive. We thus need to choose positivity, to see the good in everything- to focus on solutions rather than problems- to resist confrontations and to seek peace and harmony.

Living positively is to feel a sense of responsibility for another, for our planet, as well as other living creatures. It is to be kind, doing things outside our comfort zone. It is to approach life in a selfless manner. This transformation does not happen overnight. The object is to evolve gradually, to do a little each day. Our goal is not to escape physical reality or to become monks that meditate all day long. We need to have balance and harmony between our spiritual and physical self. Our spiritual awakening is only possible when material necessities are not the focus of our mind. The idea is not to forget about our physical needs, but rather, to elevate them. The aim is to concentrate less on our self, i.e., what I call the 'selfie syndrome', and alternatively, to think from a sharing and giving perspective, to be thankful and grateful for all we have and experience. Start the process by making small changes every day.

Do we ever question why we are who we are? All we know and all that made us who we are is rooted in our beliefs, experiences and knowledge, that were gathered through our physical senses (sight, sound, touch, taste, and smell). Consequently, our senses act as our compass and guiding light. Our ego, also known as, our outer self and conscious mind and intellect, is directing our thoughts, beliefs, and actions, solely based on suggestions we accumulate from these physical senses. Our soul, also known as, our inner self, the subconscious mind and intuition, has no say in what our senses gather and understand. In practice, we are detached from our soul, inner self, and intuition in living our daily life. We do not take the time to connect to our inner knowing. We are lacking awareness of our inner GPS and the Eternal Truth of life. Spirituality has taken a back seat to materiality. We are people that rely heavily on our conscious mind and intellect to process and deal with everything in our life. Physical reality and materialism are the center of all we know or care for most.

Have we ever taken the time to reflect on the one vital difference between a living body and a dead body? They both look the same; the only distinction is that, one no longer has the life force / soul / spirit of life within it. Therefore, the answer to the next question is obvious. Can a body live without a soul / spirit? No, it cannot. Can a body live without the ego or intellect? The answer is also obvious; yes, it can. The next logical question is at the heart of understanding the essence of mind science and the reason for our existence.

Which 'self'- ego or soul, should we consider as our life force, and consequently listen to and attend to? The answer is *our soul,* and this seems obvious, but sadly, we have lost sight of that truth. Over time, the soul was overthrown from its rightful place, and became a spiritual concept that we hardly acknowledge in our everyday life. On the other hand, our ego / intellect has taken such a central place that we think we can hardly exist without it being in charge. How foolish of us!

Further, one needs to remember that this physical body is limited to the time that the soul remains within us. Therefore, we realize the plain fact that, 'I existed as a soul before I came into this human body, and I will continue to exist as a soul after my human body is gone'. When this idea is understood, we can accept the truth that a soul that enters a physical body has a purpose or mission to accomplish. It is not here to simply spend time without any worthy objective.

A soul's purpose can only be for spiritual growth. Since, in essence, it is all spiritual and separate from physicality. It is thus, crucial to trust that each one of us has a real and good purpose for being and existing. No one's life is more important than another; we are all needed and we each have a different role to play, or mission to complete in this lifetime. Each and everyone's individual journey is precious and full of meaning.

When we connect to Infinite Intelligence, everything is possible. We can be and have all that we desire. In practice, mind science teaches us how to follow the path of least resistance, (the Divinely-guided way) in the pursuit of our goals. The idea is to connect to our spiritual self and to learn to listen to our inner being- our intuition. The ultimate test in this process and in our everyday life is to learn to overlook appearances and to see beyond the visible, into the realm of potentialities, through our *spiritual eyes.*

To overlook appearances, means that we do not focus on what our physical eyes see, but rather, we give our main attention to thinking, talking, and acting in harmony with our life's goal and purpose. We endeavor to grow spiritually and connect to the Creator in all aspects of our life. We strive to be positive and resist negativity. We make every effort to become vessels to receive all the goodness the Creator wants us to have (love, health, joy, peace, prosperity, etc...). Remember, that a full 'vessel' cannot receive much, whereas an empty one can. The goal is to stop using our ego as the primary tool to solve our apparent problems. It is the mental discipline to think in terms of solutions rather than problems. It is to teach our mind to look at everything from a constructive viewpoint. It is to stir away negative thoughts and replace them with positive ones.

We must connect to our inner GPS- the Divine sphere where everything is possible. When we do, we can experience life the way the Creator intended. The information, concepts, and conclusions in this book are shared in order to facilitate and alleviate our own individual path. The beauty of this journey is the discovery of goodness in everything and everyone. The moment we are open for change, a new world opens up to us. We are then able to embrace the Eternal Truth of life and see the endless opportunities and unlimited capabilities we all possess.

Part One
My Inner G_d

"A man is but the product of his thoughts what he thinks he becomes."

– Mahatma Gandhi

Cause and Effect

Lasting change can only come when we make a conscious decision to look inward and let go of the outer world with all of its appearances, conditions, senses, experiences and environment. Life is a continuous stream of cause and effect. We are thus unconsciously or consciously living the cause and effect of our life. The most important question we need to ask ourselves is whether we are living in *primary* cause or *secondary cause* and their respective *effects*. Do we have a main goal as the driving force of our life? Are we following a 'primary cause', or are we reacting to circumstances or appearances (which are 'secondary causes') in our life?

The law of cause and effect works whether we behave consciously or unconsciously. Whether our thoughts are random or directed, the outcome is always going to be based on our thoughts, feelings, and beliefs. To reject any natural laws- such as the laws of 'vibration', 'attraction', 'polarity', 'reciprocity', 'cause and effect' or 'primary cause and secondary cause'- does not make them less real.

To assert, 'my thoughts create my reality', is a simple concept to grasp but to actually put that concept into positive and creative action is more complex. It is necessary for any person that is at the start of their journey of self-betterment to first understand the way the mind works. Like everything in life, the creative power of our mind, or the ability to manifest something we desire must follow a blueprint, road map, or in basic terms, a 'work manual'. To achieve a desired outcome, we are required to proceed in a systematic manner. Each step can be explained in various ways, but it must persistently lead to the next step in the process of creation until our desired goal is realized or manifested. We need to be aware of the fact that once we know how the mind works, we can make better use of it, to create or change our reality. In the same vein, if we do not know how our mind works, the 'law of averages' will apply, and then, we will experience a reality that reflects random ups and downs or what we probably do not want.

Goals and Desires

The first step in the process of manifesting what we want consists in knowing what our primary goal is, and then describing it in as much detail as possible. It requires from us insightful thinking about what we truly desire and making sure that it is, in fact, what we actually want. If we express a vague desire with general statements and ambiguous words, it will not likely come into reality. We must be clear and very detailed in our own mind. The thought of our goal should provoke feelings of excitement, expectancy, fulfillment, and eagerness.

Think of it as a child anticipating a much-desired gift. The child wants that thing so much, that he can hardly keep still; he's convinced that his parents are getting it for him; it's on his mind day and night. The child never thinks or worries on the 'how' his parents are going to get it for him- only that they are. We too must have that child-like certitude that we are going to receive or achieve our goal before we actually have physical manifestation of it. We must see it in our mind first- see the result at the beginning.

Like a parent, the Creator / Infinite Intelligence will do everything to make our desire a reality. Our role is to 'think, feel and believe, and we will receive'; in spiritual terms- this means having faith in the process, never asking how or trying to figure out the way to achieve it. The idea is to have a sincere desire, to stay firm and focused on that desire, until it has manifested. In practice, this means to not give up; we must think, talk and act, in a way that only supports our desire. Any conflicting thoughts or feelings, will only damage the process of creation that we put into motion. It is important to remain unshakable, to trust the outcome, and to keep the *how* and *when* out of our mind. Do not allow the intellect to obscure what we intuitively know is possible.

Lack

When we are asking for what we desire, we must make sure that we are not asking from a place of lack, but rather, from the Eternal Truth perspective. For example, when we desire happiness or good health, because we *think* that we do not possess them, then we are thinking from a place of *lack*. This belief in lack is contrary to the Eternal Truth. It is our **Divine right** to be happy and healthy. The Creator did not bring us into this world to experience lack. We must believe this in our *thoughts*, we must express it in our *words*, and we must live it through our *actions*.

To be able to manifest our desire we have to vibrate at the frequency of creation. To attain the frequency of creation we need to live a life that is based on the Eternal Truth of life (love, kindness, peace, health, wealth, happiness, etc...). Our inner and outer being must match. If we ask Infinite Intelligence for money because we are needy, it will sense the root of the request as one of lack, and not a belief in abundance and wealth. We must believe in the Eternal Truth of life, as the Creator intended it, with no exception.

In practice, we are required to develop positive beliefs and feelings, as well as get rid of limiting beliefs, in order to vibrate at the correct (high) frequency needed for creating. To know if we are on the right frequency, we need to see what feeling our request (desire) provokes in us. If it is a good feeling- of happiness, excitement, eagerness- then we are on the right path, but if it is a feeling of doubt, fear, or anxiety, we can be sure that we are sending out the wrong vibration. The likely result will be that we will not manifest our desire because of the opposing forces at work, which are *pulling* in different directions, and in effect, are cancelling each other out. We must regularly look at the motives behind what we desire and want to manifest. Is the basis of our motive a limited belief (lack, fear, jealousy, etc...), or is it based on the Eternal Truth (abundance, health, peace, certitude, love, etc...)? This will keep us aware of our progress and what still needs work.

We must come to understand that everything in the Universe vibrates at a specific frequency. In order to manifest a particular thing, or in other words, 'attract' to us that which we desire, our energy (vibration / frequency) must vibrate at the same frequency as the thing we desire. Generally, things that we desire (love, joy, money, wealth, health) vibrate at very high frequencies. In order to attract these things in our life, we too must vibrate at these frequencies. Therefore, we need to be in an emotional state of a feel-good energy that allows 'us', the 'individual' to expand. Our subconscious mind must sense that we feel good, happy, peaceful, and in harmony- all high vibrational frequencies necessary for manifesting. We need to be or become happy and positive people in order to elevate our vibration or frequency. To reiterate, we need to let go of beliefs of lack and limitation.

The science of metaphysics explains that everything in our reality is part of the "wave-particle duality." Everything exists in a wave (energy) form before it is manifested in particulate form (physical matter). The moment our focus, attention, and thoughts are on the thing we desire to manifest, it moves from a wave state to a particle state. We are in fact putting into creative motion, from the invisible realm to the visible one, that which we desire. Science proves that when our focus is placed on something not yet physical, like the desire in our mind (i.e., what we are doing is differentiating something from the Universal Field of all possibilities), it transforms itself from a nebulous wave-like energy to a finite physical *particle*, that we are able to perceive. It takes on physical qualities. But before our attention was on that particular something- like our goal or desire, that something remains a non-physical wave of potentiality, on a continuum of an infinite stream of possibilities. The reason we are able to *see it (a particle brought into physical reality)* is that it is no longer a hazy, uncertain state of mind, or thought. In other words, it is a clear desire with focused thoughts, and feelings and energy to match.

The idea is to become skilled at using our imagination as a constructive tool for creation. Thus, 'constructive imagination', seeing the thing we desire in our mind, will take our desire out of the potential realm and bring it into the definite, physical realm. Our desire is now a real image in our mind, and coupled with will and focus will become real in our physical world. But when we think in terms of shortage, as in, 'I want money', 'I want health', or, 'I want love', and this *want* comes from a thought of, '*I don't have* money, health or love', or, 'there is not enough', or, 'it is hard', we are not believing in the Eternal Truth of Infinite Supply. One must become conscious and believe in the truth that there is no lack in the Universe. Supply of anything is infinite, including health, love, money, etc... We can all have our heart's desire. In order to see results, the Eternal Truth must first be accepted at the conscious level, and then at the subconscious level.

The idea is to think of our goal or desire as a friend. A friend is someone with whom we share many similarities. It is a person that we love, enjoy, have good times and happy moments with, etc... So, when we think of our desire or goal, it needs to make us feel good, in the same manner our friend makes us feel good. However, if the thought of our goal stirs within us feelings of stress, doubt, fear, worry or anxiety, then it is not likened to our friend and thus, we will have a hard time to attract it into our reality. In practice, this means that the idea of money should not arouse feelings of worry and stress, or finding love should not seem like a difficult thing, or make us feel undeserving or insecure. Similarly, wanting to be healthy should not seem hopeless. The goal is not to let negative emotions such as fears, along with the incorrect use of imagination, detract us from the right path to our desire. 'Destructive imagination' is simply letting our imagination think up scenarios based on fear, worry, stress, doubt, and limitations. It goes against the Eternal Truth of life. It is not real and the persistence in 'destructive imagination' can lead to the destruction of our desire. It is creating and giving force to negative energy. We need to make a conscious effort to use our imagination for what it is meant to be- a creative tool through 'constructive imagination' on the road to creation.

The Creator created this world, and everything in it, for human beings. The world, and all that which exists, is but a manifested thought, i.e., the 'primary cause' of G_d / the Creator. In the order of creation, man was created last; the heavens, the earth, the waters, the sky, the vegetation, the sun, the moon, the creatures of the sea, the birds, the animals of the land, and everything in the world, were created *first* before man.

Did we ever stop to think or ask, 'Why did this world and everything in it come into existence before man?' The creation of this world is likened to the building of a house. When we think of getting a new house built, we never think of living in that house before its completion, or while it is being built. We wait for the house to be ready- to have a foundation, walls, roof, windows, doors, running water, heat, and floors and then we bring in the furniture-, beds, tables, chairs, sofas, blankets, etc... Once the house is ready and has all that we need to live in it comfortably, we move in. Well, in the same vein, G_d- the Creator of the world and the house of man- built and furnished this world with everything man needs, before He created man. Hence, the world was created with man and his needs in mind. Once everything was in place, man was created. As such, there is no lack of supply of anything.

The only reason there is an appearance of lack is that over time we lost track of the Eternal Truth. We started giving importance to conditions, circumstances and environment, instead of remembering the original principle- that the world was created for man to live in abundance, health, joy, peace, etc... To think in terms of *need* is to affirm lack, and that is to go against the Eternal Truth and the goal of creation. For example, to manifest wealth and abundance in our life, we must always think and believe in terms that, 'I have all that I need' and, 'supply is infinite', *in spite of all appearances to the contrary.* In order to reclaim what is G_d-given and rightfully ours and to live the Eternal Truth reality, with all the good that follows, we genuinely must believe in this Eternal Truth. To experience a change in our present undesired physical reality, our thoughts, words, and actions must be aligned with the Eternal Truth reality. A good example of this truth is observable every day. Two children with similar intellectual and physical capabilities- one growing up in an affluent home- and one from a poor home. Later in life, as adults, it is common to witness that the person from the wealth-conscious home remains wealthy, while the one from the home filled with lack-consciousness, remains in lack (unless he reprograms his sub-conscious mind by believing in the Eternal Truth). The child from the wealthy home *believes* that the only way a person can or should live is affluently, because that is all he knows from his early childhood development (hetero-suggestions and affirmations from his parents, surroundings, etc..., imprinting his subconscious mind). Likewise, the adult raised in the poor home remains poor because dominant beliefs in lack are what he observed, experienced, and ultimately imprinted in his subconscious mind.

When we say that poverty, loneliness, disease etc..., is only an 'appearance' (Eternal Truth's perspective), we are bound to get resistance. At first, the idea is not simple to grasp. People are not imagining their debts or that they are sick and in pain. What they are doing is using their ego and intellect to assess and understand the situation. They are not thinking from their true self and essence- their inner self / spiritual perspective. Our soul does not know obstacles or feel pain or lack. Our soul is our connection to the Creator, the Infinite Supply of everything (love, health, wealth), but when we affirm lack or anything negative in our life, it disconnects us from the reality we want to have or deserve. When we understand this, we can have access to infinite supply with our thoughts, words, and actions. As such, when we live by this, our physical reality then changes to reflect that *Eternal Truth reality.*

However, when we live a purely physical life (based on the physical senses, conditions, and problems, rather than focusing on goals and solutions), without spiritual understanding, our physical reality will continue to reflect and keep those negative appearances as real. Be aware that Infinite Intelligence, the Creator, provides us with all that we need: health, guidance, answers, prosperity, etc... The Creator wants us to have all the good that He created for our benefit. It is our negative beliefs, interpretations, vision, and emotions that are at the root of our undesired reality. We must be open and receptive (connected) to the Creator and our G_dly soul- through our subconscious mind, in order to experience the Eternal Truth reality and to get rid of negative appearances. In practice, life will test us with obstacles, challenges, problems, and difficulties. The way we respond to these tests will reveal what beliefs we hold as true.

These tests are there to show us if we are living true to our spiritual self or to our physical self. When we have a goal / desire and until that goal is fulfilled, or has manifested, there is a time gap. The length of time for that gap can be short or long- it all depends on the individual. It will vary for each person, based on their belief, or lack thereof, in the Eternal Truth of life. During that time gap, obstacles and challenges appear to test us. Our reaction, or non-reaction, will determine our level of connection to the Creator and whether we believe in Infinite Supply.

A person that is connected to the Eternal Truth and G_d will not let the appearance of any obstacle or challenges detract him from his main goal. His belief in the Eternal Truth will remain untainted and he will not allow doubt, worry, or fear dissuade him from his goal or his faith in the Creator. Conditions, environment, or circumstances are not going to weaken his assurance and expectation in a positive outcome. The desired result or manifestation of his goal is his focus. He will think of his desire / goal as realized, and not why it cannot or will not come to be.

Obstacles and challenges are not seen as negative occurrences, but as lessons and tests to become better, stronger, and more connected to the Source of our supply. When we are connected to the Creator and are living a more spiritual life, we are able to manifest with less resistance and obstacles. We are able to accept challenges as positive experiences necessary for our growth. Any successful person in any field (sports, science, arts) will attest that the obstacles, along their path to success, have a lot to do with their great achievement. These people never see failure, defeat, and hardships as bad luck or negativity, but rather, as a way to learn, grow and become stronger and better at what they do.

On the other hand, a person that looks at these challenges, difficulties or obstacles as negative occurrences, or allow their conditions and environment to affect their mood and resolve (such as feeling depressed or hopeless), will not manifest that which they want. Moreover, when one reacts with anger, worry, fear, or resentment towards the Creator, or his circumstances and conditions, he is only empowering the negative forces or energy at work (that he himself put into motion by reacting this way in the past). Now, by again reacting the same way, he is creating more of the same for his future. **What he ends up doing is creating more of the unwanted reality and distancing himself further from reaching his goal**. Consequently, the time gap between thought-desire and fulfillment / manifestation has just widened, or worse, has indefinitely been suspended. The key to success is to keep our thoughts on what we want, chasing away opposing thoughts and stopping our intellect from giving us reasons why it is not possible or going to happen. We must remember that our supply is infinite because the source of everything is from the Creator.

I Am and I Have

When we really appreciate and accept the Eternal Truth of life, that 'supply is infinite', we no longer experience the need to think in terms of, 'I need', 'I don't have', or, 'I can't', and instead, we employ the words, 'I am', and, 'I have'. Further, when we let go of the idea of lack and correctly believe in Infinite Supply, we connect to the Creator and get to see how He, Infinite Intelligence / G_d wants to help and guide us on our path to growth. We can have all that we desire when our thoughts and actions are for positivity and for goodness. The goal is to bring the idea of 'heaven' down to earth- to infuse it in our everyday lives and not to think of it as some ideal that is somewhere far off not meant to be experienced in this physical world. Goodness, kindness, love, peace, joy, health, and abundance are the standards to live by.

Consequently, any desire we have must also reflect that Truth. Our goals have to be in accord with the Universal Laws, without abuse or selfishness, harm or ill thought towards anyone or anything. The objective is to step out of the individualistic mode of thinking and to embrace a global and universal one.

Remember that everything G_d / Source Energy created wants to serve man and be useful to him. Nature wants us to make use of it; material things want us to make use of them, but only in a way that is lifeward and good. If we train ourselves to think the way Universal Spirit / G_d intended for us to live; we realize that everything is to be used by man, but in the right way without fear of lack, worry, or that supply is limited.

Therefore, we must embrace the idea that there is no disease, lack, or obstacles in Universal Mind, but only perfect health, love, abundance, and peace. Since, I am a manifestation of Universal Mind, I, too am healthy. Disease is due to thought patterns that are opposed to the Eternal Truth reality. Thus, any thought and feeling of stress, resentment, worry, fear, doubt, anger, anxiety, hate, hostility, bitterness, etc..., is contrary to having faith and trust in the Creator, and hence, inhibits our ability to have perfect health, prosperity, and peace of mind. We need to learn to think in terms such as, 'I am peaceful and loving', or, 'I have money or money wants me', in order for us to elevate it, and we cannot think, 'I want or need money', because we fear scarcity, but rather, because we believe in Infinite Supply.

We must stop being influenced by external factors, the outer world, and conditions. We can no longer be swayed by negative thoughts; we need to strengthen ourselves and resolve to fight anything that pulls us away from our goals. We are not helpless, and we have to keep in mind that we are beings that have the power to be and have what we desire. The Creator made us with the ability to co-create anything. We only need to understand the process and connect to the Source.

As humans, with a conscious intellect and a subconscious creative power, we have the capability to grow and expand- to reach higher planes and to be better people than we were before. We are the one and only G_d creation that is able to grow spiritually, change, and evolve into something more than what it was at birth. Consequently, we must think in terms of plenty and mastery: for e.g., 'I can have all that I desire', 'I am in control of my thoughts', or, 'I am capable to do and be anything I set my mind on'. We are the ones that must influence our environment and not the reverse. We do not need to live in reactionary mode. We are required to be attentive and ready to act (with Divine guidance) on our primary goal with the certitude of its fulfillment.

Therefore, the practice of asking for what we want must be corrected and replaced by affirming and believing that **we already possess it.** This means that when we want something, we must first see it, feel it, and believe we have it in our mind. We do not communicate verbally to the Universe, or to our subconscious mind, by saying, 'I want that thing', but rather, by saying, 'I already have that thing', and by being grateful to the Creator for that thing prior to its physical manifestation. Source Energy is lifeward-moving and wants us to experience the good there is in the world (health, love, abundance, peace...).

Infinite Intelligence is within each one of us. Our physical body houses our soul. As such, the Creator would not harm our body, that He created and where He dwells. Good health is our inherent right. If we want good health, then, we need to believe that Infinite Intelligence did not make us unwell, but rather, our own negative emotions and harmful thinking did, i.e., worries, hostility, rage, stress, anxiety, fear, anger, resentment, repressed emotions, etc... Thus, we must rectify our negative thoughts and beliefs, and repeatedly affirm with certitude and confidence, 'I am healthy', or, 'I am healing everyday', because it is the lifeward way and the Divine standard. Thus, physical healing will come to us through spiritual healing, when we turn to our inner self and adhere to the Eternal Truth of life. As such, when we engage in right thinking, our good thoughts become healthy cells and our destructive thoughts become sickly and damaged cells and organs. Consequently, it is imperative to replace our destructive way of thinking with positive thinking.

When we take into account that life's movement is positive, i.e., for love, peace, harmony, health, abundance, wealth, happiness, and that there is an unlimited supply to satisfy everyone's needs and desires, it is easy to imagine and see within our mind, our desire already fulfilled, *before* it is manifested in the visible plane. This is having faith in G_d, the Creator. In practice, we are expected to ignore contrary appearances and hold steady to our affirmations and knowledge of the 'Eternal Truth'. It is the act of ignoring the present state of affairs and focusing on the story of our new desired life.

When we believe that the Creator did not create us for any negative design, or to inflict us with disease, pain, suffering, destruction, chaos, etc..., but rather, for goodness and spiritual growth, then we truly understand the purpose of creation. Do we build a house with the intent to see it as defective, damaged, or unusable to be destroyed? Similarly, do we give birth to children with the intent to see them fail, sick, or suffer; to say 'yes' would be idiotic and untrue. In the same vein, to think of life's tendencies this way or of the Creator's intent in creating this world as negative, is just simply ridiculous. The aim is not to see us fail or suffer, but rather, to see us win, to choose good over evil, and to overcome seeming challenges and to achieve success. Thus, all of the negative occurrences that we see or experience are the result of man's thoughts, beliefs, actions, uses, interpretations, and fears, etc... What we might see as failure can be a learning curve on the path to success. What we think of as punishment might be a spiritual awakening. The forces of nature are not evil or bad. Man has the choice in what manner (good or bad, negative or positive) he is going to use or interpret creation, resources, power or energy, that are at his disposal. In essence, nothing is bad, but our thinking can make it so (for e.g., the sea is not bad, but when thinking of it as being contaminated, or flooding or drowning, we then might interpret it as bad, but when thinking of it as warm, calm and having fun swimming during a summer family vacation, it is good).

Faith

The next step in the process of manifesting our goal(s) is to affirm our faith in the Creator and in our ability to co-create with Him. It is one thing to say, 'I have faith', and it is something else to *act* with faith. Faith is the ability to overlook appearances, seeming limitations (secondary cause), and to see the invisible. This means to hold a clear mental image of our goal realized, before its physical manifestation. It is the ability to say, 'I am healthy' (and believe it), even when test results say that we are seemingly not. It is the ability to say, 'I am wealthy', even when our home is being foreclosed, or to believe that we are wealthy when we have a mountain of debts. In practice, this means we must make a conscious effort to guard our thoughts and make sure that they are aligned with what we desire to manifest. It is imperative to avoid negative thoughts of what we do not want. We must block thoughts of lack or fear. We need to overlook negative appearances and to ensure that we are not unconsciously destroying / undoing / reversing / delaying what we consciously put into creative motion. Our current negative reality is a manifestation of our past negative thought patterns, but when ignored, it will enable us to experience a positive future reality.

Our role is to continually keep our focus on our desire and to deliberately ignore anything that leads to the opposite effect, such as doubt, fear, anger, anxiety, resentment, blame, limitation, or failure. The foundation of this process is *to see and to believe in the invisible* and to *overlook the visible and our apparent reality.* 'Do not judge a situation by appearances'. Further, we should not venture to 'fool' the Creator by saying that we have faith, when in truth, we are full of doubts and questions regarding how the thing we desire is going to happen, or if it is even possible. The moment we have a thought that starts with, 'yes' (I can), and then followed by a, 'but' (maybe), we are no longer in the creative plane, but are actually undoing and producing the opposite- manifesting what we fear and giving power and life to what we do not want.

In order to achieve anything in this process of manifestation, we must remember the necessity to become or be a proper vessel to create or to receive. To manifest what we desire we must think, talk, and behave in a positive and lifeward way. This means that we cannot have negative thoughts and beliefs of limitations regarding the world, people, ourselves, our current life circumstances, and / or conditions. Most of us are manifesting unwanted realities because our minds are filled with these harmful and destructive beliefs.

We manifest according to our beliefs. Thus, if we believe we can't, it's hard, it's impossible, that we're incapable, we don't deserve it, or we are unworthy, then we can be certain that our reality will match our beliefs.

In reality, what we are doing is focusing on and thinking of what happened to us in the past, or what went wrong, or who hurt us, or why we failed. We are also absorbed with our unwanted current reality and our conditions and circumstances, instead of flooding our mind with positive thoughts, having faith in seeing a positive outcome of our goals achieved.

Limited Beliefs

People are conditioned, trained, and taught from an early age to believe many inaccurate or false beliefs. For example, 'it's hard to find true love', 'you need money to make money', 'only weak people cry', 'you can't make it because...', 'nobody will love you if...', etc... These beliefs are damaging and often buried in our subconscious mind. As adults, we may not be aware of all the false beliefs that we harbor deep within us. In some cases, we cannot even recall having these beliefs. But they are there, and they are hurting our pursuit to live meaningful and fulfilled lives.

Having negative beliefs hidden in our subconscious mind is the main reason why most people are not able to manifest. Any belief that is *contrary* to our desire will damage the process of creation. Thus, we need to change these limited and harmful beliefs before we can move forward. If we do not like something in our life, or in our reality, we must take a closer look at our subconscious beliefs to find out which limited beliefs are still within us and are the root cause of our unwanted reality. We need to know which beliefs are harming us. What is stopping us from moving forward? Where is the blockage? In order to get answers, we need to be truthful, and sincerely face our beliefs about love, money, health, success, family, friendship, work, our image, forgiveness, etc...

When we uncover which limited beliefs we hold, we can then start the process to delete or replace them. Otherwise, the period between the moment we think a desired thought (goal) and the time we bring it into physical manifestation can be long and frustrating, or even worse, not at all. However, when we choose to transform our bad beliefs, or habitual thinking patterns, with the intent of adopting new positive ones, we are then making the changes necessary to manifest our desires with more ease.

To sum up, my Inner G_d is to know that there is one Creator, which is within me and is the Source of everything. In order to access Infinite Supply and to experience a positive reality, we need to believe in the Eternal Truth of life reality. In practice, it means to have *faith* in the Creator *and to believe* that He is our partner in the fulfillment of our desires.

Part Two
My Inner Power

"Once you make a decision, the universe conspires to make it happen."

-Ralph Waldo Emerson

Ego

The concept of inner power is essential to understand the process of co-creation. What is inner power? Our inner power is to know and believe that we have within ourselves the ability to co-create / manifest our sincere desire through the medium of our subconscious mind. Oftentimes, the enemy of creation is none other than our ego, which plays a big role in creating negative realities. When we listen to our ego and turn to it for solutions, we are in fact distancing ourselves from our inner power, i.e., our subconscious mind. Our subconscious mind is the link between our inner power and Infinite Supply / G_d. The reason is that our soul and Divine intelligence reside within our subconscious mind. In order to utilize our inner power, we need to let go of the ego to become proper vessels for co-creation.

The Creator / Universal Mind created us in a way that only those that look *within* are able to control their *without*. The Infinite Wisdom formed us in such a way that, to be able to find Him, we must search deep inside. When we look within, we are able to find answers, obtain solutions, and connect to our soul and to the Source of our supply. Consequently, we are able to manifest our desire.

We all possess an inner power to co-create. This power is connected to our inner G_d and is not reliant on any man or condition. Unfortunately, our individual ego often clouds our knowledge of the Eternal Truth and leads to our downfall. It is not uncommon to see many intelligent people go off course and become arrogant and self-important, and thus, disconnect from their inner G_d and inner power. The idea is to stay grounded, humble, and peaceful, in order to easily manifest that which we desire. The source of our individual power comes from our connectedness to Universal Power.

In practice, when we speak of the 'outside' we mean the use of our conscious mind / intellect and our reaction to conditions, circumstances and environment in our life. Our intellect gathers knowledge and understanding in conjunction with our physical senses (sight, smell, taste, sound, and touch). **In order to grow spiritually, we need to comprehend that our physical senses are not the only senses that are available to us.** Human physical sight, for example, is limited to the visible spectrum, but it does not deny the 'existence' of things that are invisible to the human eye like infrared light, x-rays, gamma rays, etc... It is not because we turn off the light in our room and are unable to see in the dark, that all of our furniture ceases to exist. We must recognize that if we do not see, hear, touch, smell, or taste something- that does not automatically mean it does not exist- but rather, we must keep in mind, that we are unable to perceive it with our limited physical senses. The objective is to be aware that our physical senses limit us to our physicality. However, if we are open to consider the possibility that there are other senses, like our *sixth sense*, then we can have access to endless possibilities and a wider range of perception and understanding. The idea is to accept that there are many things in the Universe that we are not aware of or that are beyond our understanding. This does not make them less real. The more open we are, the more perceptive and receptive we become.

When we live true to our essence (connected to our soul, to Infinite Supply and our intuition) and when we follow the natural laws of the Universe, we are able to co-create. We are all required to follow a path of growth, of striving to be better and better each day. We must live according to the laws of creation, which are only positive. Everything is for our good- we must think it and believe it. It is important to wish well for others. It is essential to rejoice in others' accomplishments, and when possible, even help them on their road to success. This also holds true for people we do not like, or even consider our seeming competitors.

We must train our mind to think on the creative plane and not on the competitive plane. Since there is no lack and supply is infinite, we must let go of the fears of scarcity and the need to compete. We must send out thoughts of love, blessings, and peace, and in the process, become positive individuals. This, in turn will press forward positive effects in our own life. If we really believe in the Creator and the power of the Universal Mind to create anything that we desire, we can then, embrace the notion of everything is for the good and in abundant supply, with certainty that there is plenty to go around. It is to understand that if I have plenty, it's not at the detriment of anyone; it does not mean that someone else has to have less. Supply is not dependent on any person, condition, or environment. The need to compete is then, unnecessary.

The desired progress and the change in our behavior can be gradual; small positive acts (smiling, helping, giving, kindness, love, forgiveness...) daily can produce great transformations over time. It is important to do our best to achieve harmony from within and from without in order to be successful. As part of the 'One Source', we are all connected, and thus, we all have a global responsibility to think and act with global consciousness. The thought of 'me, myself and I' has no place in this process. We are to think in terms of, 'my desire is not above or at the detriment of another'. When we live by that truth, all that we need or desire is easily attained.

When spirituality is included in our daily life we have better access to our inner power. Our intellect / ego will try to keep us away from our inner G_d and inner power, but having awareness of this, enables us to not let it detract us from accessing and benefiting from it.

Our Mind

There are two primary powers of the mind that lead a man to grow spiritually. One is the *power of the intellect* and the other is the *power of the heart*. When we say, 'power of the intellect', we refer to our *conscious mind*; when we say, 'power of the heart', we mean a feeling or a sensation- our *subconscious / super-conscious mind*. Before we go further on the topic of mind power, it is important to first comprehend how our mind works. In simplistic terms, we all have a mind that has essentially two distinct functions known as, (1) *the conscious mind* and (2) the *subconscious* mind. Some experts in the study of mind science add a *third* function of the mind called 'supra-conscious' or 'super-conscious' mind. However, in this book, it is referred to as, 'Divine intelligence' (see section, 'Physical Intelligence & Divine Intelligence', below). Here, it is treated as part of the subconscious mind, with its own distinct functions.

The conscious mind is our intellect and its ability to reason, to process, select, compare, and analyze through our physical senses of smell, touch, sight, sound, and taste. Our conscious mind is *deductive and inductive* in nature; it will deduce and induce conclusions, beliefs, and affirmations from knowledge, facts, and experiences. It is influenced by the *outside* world. It is often referred to as, the 'master' or the 'captain' of our mental 'ship'.

Our subconscious mind is our *creative* mind; it does not use intellect, but rather, it uses *hetero* ('by others') or *autosuggestion* ('by ourselves') and intuition as its compass. It uses *ONLY DEDUCTIVE processes* to arrive at conclusions based on what it has gathered from the conscious mind. It is *only* amenable to suggestions given to it. Thus, it only deals with information that already exists and previously stored in its memory bank. The subconscious mind, because of its deductive nature, cannot differentiate between what is imaginary and what is real, or what is true and what is false, or what is good and what is bad. It is our inner voice that needs our direction, to know what we want it to do. In practice, this means, it follows what our intellect believes and allows in. It organizes the information gathered into categories, such as, fear, happiness, wealth, success, health, love, etc... Our subconscious mind is powerful, because it has the unique power to co-create. However, it is also blind and 'a follower', and therefore, requires our conscious guidance. Again, it is deductive only and it is the home to all of our memories, feelings, and original beliefs. The subconscious mind (a.k.a. unconscious mind or subjective mind) does not differentiate between right and wrong and truth from non-truth. If we believe in things that are not good, positive, or true, it cannot reject them. It reads *emotions*- how our beliefs make us *feel*. It understands sensations, moods, and feelings; it takes for truth whatever the conscious mind, as the guardian of the subconscious mind, allows in. When our conscious mind fills our subconscious mind with negative limited beliefs, our subconscious mind has no way to know it is a limited or false belief. Further, it has no other alternative than to accept these limited beliefs, since the 'captain' (the conscious process of our mind) commanded it so, and as a result, over time the subconscious mind is filled with suggestions from which it creates a reality to match. It only creates from what it has already received from the conscious mind and is already stored within itself. It cannot gather information independently.

Remember, our subconscious mind is impersonal; it does not have a thinking and reasoning capability- a process or possibility to choose or decide. It only works with what it was told and with which it was imprinted. It follows the command of the master and captain, i.e., the conscious mind. That is why it is called, the 'SUB-conscious' mind, since it is below, under the control or 'SUB-ject' to our conscious mind. At birth, our subconscious mind is a blank page, ignorant and uninformed and dependent on the conscious mind to enlighten it, to fill its 'empty space'. From the moment we are born, our subconscious mind is subject to sounds and images. As we grow, so does our bank of limited beliefs. As such, to be able to manifest a healthy, happy, and prosperous life, our subconscious mind must have more information and beliefs that reflect and stir feelings of joy and abundance, than those of lack and sadness. It cannot have in its bank of memories anything that supports conflicting or opposing views and emotions to the ones we want to manifest.

Unfortunately, most of us have been brainwashed to believe many false and limiting beliefs, and consequently, our subconscious mind is full of these damaging beliefs. This is the core reason why most people have difficulty in manifesting their goals and dreams. Since thoughts of lack, poverty, fear, and hardship are so common, they give rise to negative feelings, which in turn, create unwanted results and realities. In practice, what happens is, that we respond to these apparent realities, (instead of ignoring them and concentrating on what we do want to manifest), and as a result, we end up creating more of the same unwanted reality. It is a recurrent circle of the same thoughts / behaviors that lead to the same results. Consequently, to break away from this unwanted pattern, any new thought we have should *ideally* arise from the Universe of infinite potential thoughts and possibilities (wave / particle duality). But, in reality, most of our new thoughts are born from what is already stored in our subconscious mind. Thus, our *seemingly* 'new' thoughts are born out of our old-established beliefs and patterns, from the known spectrum in our subconscious mind (whether good or bad, positive or negative), i.e., our habits. In essence, our new thoughts are nothing new, but only a reflection of our old thoughts, words, and actions. Further, those allegedly new thoughts are always in harmony with our subconscious mind's beliefs. **Therefore, to step away and to break the cycle of repeated unwanted thoughts and realities, we need to adopt new and different beliefs.** For that to happen we must replace our existing limiting beliefs and patterns, which are lodged within our subconscious mind, with new thoughts that are not yet known to it *and are in harmony with the Eternal Truth of life.*

We have to step out of our comfort zone and delve into the unknown in order to adopt new beliefs and to form new habits. In practice, we need to expose ourselves to new ideas and experiences. This, in turn, will allow us to generate new positive thoughts that will let us manifest a different, albeit, desired reality. The idea is to break the known habit and to travel on a new road, totally unknown to us. The mechanics to changing our negative and unwanted thought patterns, in brief, is to think new thoughts from outside our spectrum of old thoughts. Through will, focus, and repetition of these new positive thoughts, we will imprint new beliefs and create new positive habits. The techniques to assist us to achieve change in our beliefs will be discussed in the third part of this book, titled, 'Inner Solution'.

To attain success in the creative process of manifesting, it is necessary to grasp this point well. To reiterate, when our focus and reaction is on our seeming reality, (the outside world, circumstances, secondary cause) instead of focusing on our desire / main goal in life (primary cause), the outcome will always be a recurrence of the same unwanted reality. When we think of what we do not want, instead of what we do want, what we witness is a repeat performance, a recurring cycle of negative creation.

In practice, when we wake up in the morning unhappy because our reality and apparent conditions are bad and intolerable, we can react in one of two ways: negatively or positively. Typically, people react by getting angry, upset, frustrated, fed up, feeling sorry for themselves, thinking how unfair it is, etc...

The positive and necessary way to act, in order to stop this reality from continuing or recurring, is to put aside the seemingly bad reality and to choose to overlook it. This means we are taking charge of our thoughts, by directing them away from the undesired reality, and replacing them with positive thoughts, of things we desire or love, even if at first it might seem hard to do. Nonetheless, if we make the effort and apply it, it gets easier. Hence, in spite of all the seeming difficulties, it is crucial to remember the way in which the mind works. We need to take control of our thoughts and move them to a feel-good place. It takes work at first, like learning to swim, bike or walk, but it becomes effortless with practice. What we want to do is guide our thoughts in the right direction away from our current reality. This also applies to steering our talk and our actions towards what we desire and to avoid anything that is to the contrary.

We must understand that in order to stop repeating the same unwanted reality, it is vital to think and focus on what we want in our future, and totally *ignore* our present reality. We need to have faith in the process and to believe we are going to manifest our desire. To implement that, we need to wake up in the morning and to choose to think of our desired goal, and consequently, to say (even robotically) our positive affirmations that support our goal. We must think of and feel our desire / goal with intensity and consistency. The test is to refuse to give in to temptation and to revert to familiar old thoughts, language, and acts that are negative and that relate to our present condition. As such, we should never say, 'I have no life', 'I am alone', 'I do not feel good', 'I have debts', 'I am sick', 'I am unhappy', 'I am depressed', 'I am broke', etc... We must avoid this impulse, even if it reflects our present reality. The only thing we are accomplishing by talking about our apparent reality is the creation of more of the same. We may experience temporary relief by talking about our problems, challenges, or negative experiences. We might think it is good to get things 'off our chest', but be assured that the 'relief' is short-lived and comes at a tremendous cost to us, **since we are recreating the same undesired reality**.

It is crucial to break our old patterns in order to move forward. It is indispensable to identify what is blocking us, or to uncover what harmful beliefs we are harboring, and why we feel this way. Once we are able to identify the root cause of these destructive beliefs, we are then expected to deal with them, or eliminate them, before we can truly move on and manifest anything. In practice, we need discipline to stay strong and resist the urge to think about and focus on our present reality. We must work on eliminating our negative thoughts, beliefs, and ignore secondary causes, i.e., environment, conditions, and circumstances. The subconscious mind is the 'magic wand' that *creates* for us, and the conscious mind is the 'magician' that *gives the* wand *directions*. The 'magic wand' has all the power of creation, but cannot apply it without the helping hand of the 'magician' / 'master'.

In other words, it requires teamwork between the conscious and subconscious minds. Our conscious mind must give attention to the thoughts / desires we do want to manifest, along with seeing or imagining them with details and accuracy, (in our mind and in the invisible plane), before they have manifested. That, in turn, will lead to the creation of a *prototype* of our desire in the *invisible sphere*, where that desire and 'spiritual order' is ready for delivery from the 'spiritual warehouse' of Infinite Supply. To move the prototype from the invisible plane to the visible physical plane, our subconscious mind needs to *believe and feel* that it is really what we want. For this to come about, a corresponding *positive emotion* must be *attached* to that thought-desire. Once this is accomplished, we keep our focus on our desire, until it manifests on the physical plane.

In practice, this means that our subconscious mind will come across the prototype (of our desire), and give us a response deep-rooted in beliefs stored in its memory bank. If our *beliefs* and desired goal *match* the *feelings and emotions* found in our subconscious storehouse, it will *respond positively*, since the subconscious mind has no other choice but to bring it into being. However, if there is no match with what we have in our subconscious storehouse, then it will simply resist or refuse to manifest for us what we ask. We then have to remove the limiting beliefs that are blocking our creative process. Our conscious mind needs to bring about the necessary change in beliefs, since the change must first occur on the conscious level. Our conscious mind adopts new beliefs and rejects the old ones, in order to impress the subconscious mind with these new beliefs. **If we do this with *persistence and repetition*, then the subconscious mind will let go of the old beliefs and simultaneously imprint new ones.** Remember, repetition is the key to success.

Physical Intelligence & Divine Intelligence

We all possess a *physical intelligence* and a *Divine intelligence*. Physical intelligence resides within our conscious mind, and Divine intelligence is found within our subconscious mind. Some authors refer to this Divine intelligence as the *'supra-conscious'* mind- a third and distinct function of the mind. However one wishes to classify this particular function of the mind, the function nevertheless remains the same.

To manifest our desires, it is essential to allow Divine intelligence to guide us; however, most of us rely heavily on the use of our Physical intelligence for our day-to-day functioning.

Physical intelligence, a.k.a., our "intellect", has its source in our *physical senses* (sight, sound, touch, taste, and smell). From these senses, our physical intelligence decides, judges, perceives, limits, observes, induces, deduces, analyzes, investigates, concludes, challenges, questions, doubts, agrees, assesses, dissects, absorbs, translates, processes, weighs, understands, learns, rationalizes, interprets, accepts, rejects, thinks, forms opinions, etc... Physical intelligence is part of our conscious mind. It is the *thinking* part of our mind.

Divine intelligence is our *intuitive intelligence* that has its source in Infinite Intelligence- the Creator. It is our 'spirit' and a part of our subconscious mind. It can be characterized as infinite, unbounded, supra-intelligence, Divine, supra-natural, limitless, it knows the truth, it knows only goodness, it is life-giving, supra-rational, all-knowing, it is G_dliness, it keeps us alive without any assistance from our intellect (see *'Original Beliefs'* above).

People who wish to find Divine intelligence need to turn *inwardly* and to 'quiet' their Physical intelligence in order to *listen* to their Divine intelligence. The quieter our mind is, the more connected we will be to Divine intelligence, and the more we can access the answers, solutions and outcomes we are seeking.

Divine intelligence will help us when we call upon it, *provided that our Physical intelligence does not interfere* (by negatively controlling and influencing our subconscious mind), but rather *defers* to the power of Divine intelligence (also *via* our subconscious mind). If our subconscious mind is filled with limited beliefs, it is the result of our Physical intelligence *influencing* and *controlling* our subconscious mind, and therefore, our Divine intelligence will not generate for us *intuitive information or solutions* since the beliefs we hold are not in harmony with the Eternal Truth of Divine intelligence. Our subconscious mind, via our 'soul', is the *link between our conscious mind and our Divine intelligence, (or supra-conscious mind).* Divine intelligence will not impose itself on us. When we have a sincere desire to let go of our limited beliefs and we decide to change, this is when our Divine intelligence, upon our request, will provide us with supra-intelligent / intuitive solutions.

When we allow this process to occur, solutions, answers, positive manifestations and assistance will come forth (albeit, in its own time). The 'how' and 'when' this happens, is not the function of our Physical intelligence, but of Infinite Intelligence, and therefore, we must not attempt to control these parameters. This is to have faith in the process. The moment we try to be in charge, we are interfering with the laws of creation and Divine intelligence. The Creator (like a parent) wants to help, guide, and provide us with what we need. We must only realize this and turn to Infinite Intelligence within us.

Individual Creative Power

The way an individual manifests things into reality, for e.g., success, a home, good health, love, etc..., works in the same way that the Universal Creative Power creates things, for e.g., a tree, a mountain, a lake, etc...(albeit on a micro-scale). Their main characteristics are the same: the nature of this power is infinite, neither time nor space-bound and undifferentiated (it is not describable as any particular thing because it is the potentiality and / or actuality of anything and everything in the Universe at any given space and / or time). Going one step further, once something has been brought into creation, either by the Universal Creative Power or by our Individual Creative Power (by thinking it over and over), the thing created is *both* differentiated (time and space bound), but is simultaneously a part of the *Undifferentiated Universal Substance.* Even though Universal Substance (a.k.a. Original Substance / G_d) differentiates many things in the Universe (people, nature, things, etc...), the Universal Substance is not in the least diminished by its differentiating power. Everything we desire already exists in the Universe, and the fact that the human eye does not see it on the visible plane does not mean it is not there. All things are created and come from the Undifferentiated Original Substance. Our individual thought (our will) comes into physical form as Individualized Differentiated Substance that is from and part of the Universal Undifferentiated Substance. Think of the Universe and the Universal Undifferentiated Substance as one big circle, with everything we want, existing inside the circle. The Individualized Universal Substance is a tiny piece inside the circle that is differentiated, but nonetheless, still remains a part of it. Keep in mind that the *entire* 'area' of the 'Big Circle' of the Universal Undifferentiated Substance remains *completely undifferentiated* as mentioned above. In other words, creating / co-creating something from Universal Substance, does not diminish its supply; its nature remains unlimited and infinite. The idea is to always keep in mind that we are connected to G_d / Universal Spirit- the Source of everything.

Another way to understand this is to know that the Universe is one big energy field. Everything in the world is energy. Everything we see and everything we do not see is energy. When we speak of energy, we also refer to vibration and frequency. We are all vibrating beings. To the naked eye it appears that we are all different shapes of mass and substance. However, in reality, everything from a human being to a seemingly inanimate object, like a stone, is energy arranged and vibrating at extremely high, but different frequencies.

The reason why we are able to, or unable to manifest, depends on the frequency on which we are vibrating. Since everything is energy, a certain energy frequency *within us* is needed for the creation of our desire (for e.g., money, health, love, car, home, all vibrate at a certain frequency). Thus, when we vibrate at the *same frequency* as that of the thing we desire, we can manifest that thing. The 'prerequisite' to manifesting is to feel good and be positive in order to emanate high energy, or a higher vibrational frequency within us. This condition is **necessary** to manifesting any desire. To reach a high-energy frequency, the individual must be in a peaceful, happy, upbeat, and positive frame of mind, i.e., the way the Creator intended for us to live. At the opposite end of this, we have a negative, depressed, critical, unhappy, angry, snappy, and sad individual that is vibrating at a *low* frequency, with no power to manifest anything positive. Do not expect life to take on a positive twist if our mind remains negative and unchanged. Consequently, the negative individual will not manifest his desires, since he is living contrary to the Eternal Truth. This is true even if he is applying razor sharp focus on his desired goal. To successfully manifest, the individual must be in harmony (thought, desire, emotion) in order to match the '*vibration of creation*'. Thus, the rate at which we are transmitting energy will determine if we are able to manifest what we want.

Since we are always manifesting wanted or unwanted realities, it is important to reach the right frequency to manifest what we want and not some unwanted outcome or reality. When we are unhappy with our reality, we can be sure that we are not vibrating at the right frequency for creation. In practice, this means that we must elevate our frequency, by changing our attitude, mood, and feelings. The way to achieve results is to become happy positive people. Thus, we are required to eliminate our negative beliefs and change our attitude since they are keeping us away from any real progress. The moment we get rid of the negative influences, positivity is able to permeate our whole being.

To begin the process of changing the old negative beliefs that reside within our subconscious mind, we must *repeat incessantly* our new positive thoughts, words, and actions until they are drummed into the subconscious mind. Consequently, the subconscious mind will let go of these old unwanted thoughts, and replace them with new positive ones. They then become new (desired) beliefs, within our subconscious mind. A thought that is repeated often to oneself ('autosuggestion') will eventually become a belief (i.e., accepted by our subconscious mind).

Our feelings, vibrations, energies are also a reflection of our thoughts. Hence, if we are thinking positive thoughts (most of the time), then we are supposed to feel good and happy, and our energy and vibrational frequency ought to be high and positive. As opposed to when we are thinking negative thoughts, or expressing limited beliefs, and as a result, our vibration / frequency level is low.

One can take comfort in the fact that no two thoughts can occupy the mind at the same time. Thus, the secret to fighting and eliminating a negative thought lies in catching the negative thought and making a conscious choice to replace it with a positive one. At first, it might seem overwhelming and difficult to manage our thoughts, but with practice and perseverance, it becomes easy and even automatic. We should **start to think about what we think about most**. In practice, it is easy to discover a negative pattern of thinking.

If our new thought-desire (that we want to impress upon our subconscious mind) does not create a positive emotion and a corresponding good feeling, it means that our conscious mind and subconscious mind are not in harmony. We can then assume that there are limited or contradictory beliefs we are not consciously aware of, and that are still within our subconscious mind. That is the reason why we are not experiencing positivity or feeling good. In fact, what we realize is that our subconscious mind has not yet replaced the old limited beliefs with the new thought-desire. In practice, we want to adopt a new belief and our intellect and conscious mind leads the way for this new belief. But in actuality, our subconscious mind has not yet accepted our new thought-desire. The issue that our mind is facing is- that this new conscious thought / belief we want to impress our subconscious mind with, goes against what we believed in our past. Our old belief that we wish to replace, is still stored in our subconscious mind, and thus, there is a clash between the new belief and the old one. **This means that to imprint the subconscious mind with a new belief we need to work at it with persistence and patience.** We must incessantly repeat the new thought-desire until the subconscious mind *'believes' us.* It needs to *feel our sincerity* before it will accept this thought as a new belief.

The objective is to reach a state where thoughts and feelings match. If I say, 'I am happy', I must feel happy, but if my feeling is not of happiness, then the creative power will not work within me or through me, because it senses that I am not being truthful. Our subconscious mind will not go against something it does not believe we truly want. The only way it knows the truth, is through our *feelings* and *emotions*. It will sense our happiness and excitement or our fear and doubt to determine what we truly believe.

Our physical senses are the mechanism through which the conscious mind uses to form beliefs, to have life experiences and to obtain knowledge. From the time we were babies- what we saw, heard, touched, tasted and smelled- was collected, gathered, processed and accepted by our conscious / objective mind and stored and conserved in our subconscious / subjective mind. As such, our subconscious mind is fully loaded with memories, beliefs, and suggestions that are true as well as false.

As adults, and even as children, we are held back due to our limited, negative, hurtful, and destructive beliefs. We are, therefore, unable to bring forth the change for which we long. Our reality remains unchanged until the moment these negative beliefs are replaced with beneficial, positive, and constructive ones. Our daily reality is the direct outcome of having these beliefs. For example, if I believe I cannot do something, the Universe will give me many reasons for why I cannot do this. If I always complain about things, the Universe will find for me many more situations about which to complain. If I am unhappy, my reality will find reasons for me not to be happy. Recurring thoughts become our reality. Positive thoughts become a positive reality. Negative thoughts become a negative reality. Thus, it is important to guard our thoughts, in order to experience a desired reality, rather than, an undesired one.

Looking Inward

In our pursuit to transform our self and our reality, we are expected to look inward to our inner self, and there we will find all that we need to consider for the transformation and improvement we are seeking. Change will come when we look inward and not outward for the solutions. In order to bring about noticeable change, we must try new things. The idea is to explore new avenues, and delve into the unknown. Often times, we hold onto our old ways because it is all we know. We prefer to stay within the confines of the known, rather than face new horizons. The fear of the unknown is often the reason that prevents us from uncovering the genius within. This destructive fear deters us from moving toward something so much better. Oftentimes, we resist change, even if it is for our own good. It is a very old survival mechanism that our subconscious mind employs to keep the *status quo.* If we honestly aspire to change our reality, we are required to think and act differently from our past ways. We are obligated to push ourselves to think outside our habitual way. We should create a little disturbance in our patterns and customary ways of thinking. This will lead us to ask ourselves some deep existential questions like:

⇒ 'What's my life's purpose?'

⇒ 'Why do I exist?'

⇒ 'Am I destined to live a life of fear, unhappiness and mediocrity?'

⇒ 'Is this what the Creator intended for me-or am I able to be more?'

⇒ 'Is the pursuit of material good the only purpose I have?'

⇒ 'How do I make a difference in this world and not simply exist?'

The Creator made us in such a way that we are all able to make a positive difference in this world. We humans are the crown of creation; we are equipped with tools no other creation has. Human beings have the ability to use their mind, intellect, intuition, and creative power to shape and change their life. We also have free will to choose between being good or not good. Our capacity to make a difference in this world- to help others, to always strive to improve, to be forward thinkers, to spread love, goodness, kindness, peace- are basic norms, and not some grand ideals.

If we are not willing to break free of our old superficial ways, and to start living a more meaningful life that we were born to live, then we will remain prisoners of our own doing, chained to these old beliefs. We are the only ones responsible for our lives and the only ones that can break these chains. The Creator gave us the tools to transform and grow. We are the ones that hold the key to our own freedom. We need to consciously want to take control of our life and be free again- as free as children. To achieve this, we must embrace new thoughts and create new feelings. We must understand the way our mind works, to be able to bring about our desired transformation. What we know and what we frequently think about must change, if it has not produced the reality we desire. **Thus, if we are unhappy with our reality and do not like what we see in our life, then something is definitely wrong with our habitual thinking pattern.** Our life is the '*compass*' that lets us know if we are thinking in the right direction or not, it is the mirror of our thoughts. Thus, in order to see desired results, we must give rise to a new course, drive on a new road- one that leads us to new destinations and leaves the old ones behind.

By now, we can all appreciate that to experience new results we must change the direction of our thoughts. For that, we need to make significant modifications in our thinking patterns, which in turn lead us to alter our spoken words, and further, our actions. If we do not commit to replace our habitual way of doing things, then we will not bring about any real and lasting transformation in our reality.

Everything we experience in this world on the material plane is an *exact* reflection and replication of what we think and believe within our subconscious mind. To change our life, i.e., what we experience in this physical world, we need to change our thoughts and beliefs. This requires consistent daily mental discipline to re-condition our mind, same as when we go to the gym to re-condition our body. It is wrong to look at the circumstances in our life and to think that they are happening to us from some outside source. In reality, we make them happen with our own thoughts and beliefs. Where our thoughts go, energy flows, and where our energy flows reality goes. We must remember that our thoughts have feelings, those feelings vibrate at a certain frequency, and in turn, that frequency determines the energy we send out. When the frequency is high or aligned with our desire we manifest a wanted reality. Consequently, if we are serious about improving our life and are ready and willing to make the necessary modifications, then the process outlined in this book will help us achieve what we long for. Some may think that this is a tall order to carry out, but it is not; it is as simple or as complicated as we want it to be- like everything, it is all in our mind.

Self-Change

The first thing we must do on the road to change, is to consciously pay attention and make sure we no longer think, speak and act negatively, in our regular habitual way. We need to change our bad habits, actions, and patterns. We must do this on the conscious level, in order to experience change on the subconscious level. Do not assume that positive change can occur with our old negative ways untouched. In order to break the pattern, we need to do things differently, to surprise our subconscious mind with new ideas and a new 'me'. The objective is to create new beliefs and behaviors that our subconscious mind does not recognize and does not know. This new 'me' means we start acting outside our habitual way; our subconscious mind will not know what to do, and will not recognize these new thoughts and behaviors. Thus, our subconscious mind will start imprinting new suggestions. This does not mean that our old beliefs are necessarily gone as soon as we start. It means that we have new thoughts in our subconscious mind. The same goes for our new behaviors and patterns; they will also enter our subconscious mind. To experience change, the quantity of thoughts, words, actions, and emotions we transmit to our subconscious must be incessant and frequent in order to confront and replace our unwanted ones.

We must persist in this practice until it becomes our new habit. Once the new pattern is accepted by the subconscious mind, it is a new, different, and permanent belief from which new manifestations are born.

In practice, it is essential to take responsibility for our life by not blaming anyone or anything for our seemingly negative reality, such as, circumstances and environment. When we let go of blame then we have begun the process of creating a new and better reality. When we look at our life and understand, as well as accept, that everything in it is a consequence of our thinking, believing, and acting, then we are in fact admitting to our past mistakes. This is a sure sign that we are on the right path to realizing our goals. Just as it is our own doing that created this reality, likewise, our own undoing will bring the desired change.

Our future can be different. We no longer need to be victims of circumstances (secondary cause). We do not have to live average lives, always reacting and not being in control. We must have faith and *believe* in the process of manifesting. **Our mind, through its subconscious faculty, is able to do and be whatever we want.** Our 'machine'; i.e., body, mind and soul, is designed this way. Once we think a thought *recurrently*, our subconscious mind will react to it and take action according to the existing beliefs it has within it. The aim is to impress the subconscious mind by letting it know exactly what we desire, with faith and constancy, as well as trust in the outcome, and then we *must* step aside, and wait; we should *not force* the process upon it. The Universe, i.e., the Creator, will handle the details, the 'how and when'. The Creator will send us 'indicators' of how we should participate in the process of co-creating. If any action is required of us, besides keeping our focus on our goal, Infinite Intelligence will let us know.

By illustration, a businessperson that needs assets to sustain his business will do the following: he will ask the Universe to send him answers to the questions of how and from whom he should get the assets? He asks Divine intelligence within him for guidance, by stating his request with as many details as possible. He can say, 'Infinite Intelligence I need [he states a certain $ amount here] to expand my warehouse; the business is growing and I need more space to accommodate the growth. Please direct me and show me what I must do to achieve my goal'. He further asks the Creator for directives, in finding the right location for his warehouse. He can also ask to meet the right people to work with. He says, 'Infinite Intelligence please direct me to the right location', he then can ask for assistance between two or three locations he has in mind or he can ask to be directed to a totally new location. He has *faith* and *knows* that the Universe will respond to his request. The Universe will send 'signs', provide encounters, hunches, a gut feeling, insights, and intuition. He affirms with confidence that, 'Infinite Intelligence guides and directs me in all my business endeavors and shows me what I am required to do. Infinite Intelligence also puts on my path people that are honest and loyal and that know my business.' He then, lets go of the 'how' and 'when' the funds or answers will come. It is not for him to come up with the solutions. The Universe responds to him at the right time with all he needs through intuitive leads- ideas, thoughts, and assistance from unexpected people- none of which was facilitated by him, but rather, by the Creator. He is Divinely guided throughout the process. When following this course of action, we are amazed by the speed and precision of its response. It is imperative that one must remain **steadfast** in his request until the answers come. This is what it means to have singularity of purpose or a **focused** mind. Think of it as giving precise instructions to our personal magic wand, and in return, it gives us an exact response to our command.

To better understand the way of manifesting our desired life, we must first accept the Creator as our Partner. The link to our Partner is our subconscious mind and Divine intelligence. Our spiritual self, our soul, is part of the Creator, and through our subconscious mind, we are vessels to receive Divine guidance.

This means that in practice, the first thing we must do is to ensure that our subconscious mind believes (through the portal of our conscious mind) the one essential Eternal Truth- that there is a Universal Creator (a/k/a G_d / Infinite Intelligence / Source Energy / Infinite Power / Universal Spirit / Universal Mind / Infinite Wisdom / Universal Substance / Infinite Supply) that created us and everything else. We must embrace this idea, that there is something larger than us. *We must believe it.* **If we are unable to internalize this fundamental Eternal Truth of a 'Creator', then we will not be able to connect and depend on our inner G_d and our inner power to create through our subconscious mind.** It is pure arrogance and ignorance on our part to think that there is nothing greater than us. Holding that sort of belief only hurts, delays, and hinders our ability to bring forth the life we want.

What does it mean to believe in something greater than us?

The Creator

It means to believe in the Creator, and that He created us as intelligent beings, with our own power to co-create, because each individual is a microcosm of the Creator. We are made in the image of the Creator. The Creator is infinite- not limited. He is everywhere and in everything. He is defined neither by time nor by space. Just as our physical bodies resemble our biological parents, so too does our spiritual self resemble our Spiritual Parent / G_d / the Creator. We are all part of this One G_d / Creator / Original Source / Divine intelligence, and as such, we are all connected to each other and to the One Universal Power / Source Energy / G_d.

In practice, this means that only the people that are aware of their connection to Universal Intelligence are also aware that He empowers them- their mind and their subconscious self- with the ability to take charge of their life and their thoughts, and bring into physical form their desires. We must learn to understand our inner self and to listen to our inner voice. Consequently, this means that our physical self serves our spiritual self and not the opposite. We are now in control, not being controlled. Our life does not need to be the result of random unorganized thoughts and beliefs.

We must train ourselves not to allow externalities and our environment to affect us, but rather, become the ones that affect our environment. We must become receptive to all possibilities and to transcend the limitations of the physical realm. We must tap into our invisible powers that come from our intuition and spiritual growth. Our individual subjective mind is linked to the Universal Subjective Mind, which guides and directs our actions, in order to attain what we need and want. We are then able to co-create our reality. Or specifically, we are allowing the Creator to direct and express His instructions to create *through* us. We are fulfilling the Divine will through our extrasensory perception (E.S.P.), or intuition. This course of action is only possible if we have faith. This power, which is within us, is available to everyone without exception, and is not dependent on physical intelligence, talent, nationality, religion, etc... It becomes more apparent as our faith becomes stronger.

Faith as the Connector

Faith is the ability to see, believe, and expect the invisible. Faith is what allows us to know for sure we are *already in possession* of what we desire *before* we have it. Our thoughts, blended with faith in the Creator / Infinite Intelligence, will bring forth the realization of our goals. **Faith is the *connector* to Infinite Intelligence and the spiritual link to receiving.** When we have faith, we connect to the Source of our supply, and we are able to see and expect the result before it becomes visible. The outcome of having faith, on the practical plane, can come in the form of 'signs', intuition, hunches, directives and guidelines- a peaceful sense of knowing what we must do (actions) and the steps we must follow to manifest our desires.

The moment we have faith, everything falls into place. Things begin to align themselves and goal-oriented situations occur- all with the purpose to lead us to our goals. People with faith are serene, peaceful, and positive; they are not anxious, afraid, or doubtful. That is the reason why people with faith see their prayers answered, because in their heart and subconscious mind they truly *believe* their prayers are going to be answered. They *expect* the outcome of their desires. They see the end at the beginning.

People with faith have peaceful and loving personalities that are aligned with their positive and high energy / vibration, which in turn, enables them to receive / co-create without delay. Our inner creative power, also known as Infinite Intelligence *within* our subconscious mind, needs to connect to Universal Infinite Intelligence to manifest our desires. Doing this sends our request to Universal Infinite Intelligence that creates for us or through us.

Keep in mind that when we are connecting to Universal Infinite Intelligence, our *feeling* / energy / vibration *must match* our request. Infinite Intelligence within our subconscious mind knows and senses *how we feel,* and as such, we cannot pretend to feel positive, and then expect our desired results to manifest. We must genuinely feel positive, loving, happy, serene, peaceful, joyful, content, abundant, prosperous, grateful, etc... **We must make sure that positive emotions are dominating our mind.** *Emotions and feelings*, **along with** *faith*, **are the language our subconscious mind understands.** The aim is to feel good and positive in order to send out the right emotions and feelings needed for co-creation. All this is possible with some effort on our part and with a true desire for change.

As soon as we start to alter our thoughts, speech, actions, feelings and beliefs, our subconscious mind has no choice but to comply with our desires. Our subconscious mind does not have the power to reason or decide, but can only follow orders based on what it has collected and is familiar with and knows. All this may seem overwhelming at first, but in reality, once the process is in motion the transformation happens like the 'snowball effect'. One thing leads to the next; the main thing is to just start. Once we do, we will see things change; new thoughts lead to new emotions and beliefs, which in turn, lead to more good feelings and emotions that result in positive change.

The process can be as short or as long as the time it takes for each one of us to clear our subconscious mind; we must get rid of our limited beliefs and adopt and bring into being new ones. Some limited beliefs will be replaced easily, and some will need more work. It all depends on how strong a hold that belief has on our subconscious mind. The objective is to stay on course, and to keep doing confidently what is needed, until we reach our goal.

Love Yourself

Love is the most powerful and motivating emotion. When we feel love and when we send out love, we are able to conquer all. What has not been done or claimed in the name of love? Love is part of the Eternal Truth and at the root of everything. 'Love your neighbor as you love yourself'- there is no better way to live than by that truth. To vibrate at the frequency of love, we have to make sure we have no hidden, unwanted, or damaging beliefs regarding love.

We must start this process with a true understanding that love is crucial for our self-growth. When we speak of love, we first speak of self-love. 'How am I going to send out loving thoughts and energy if I don't truly love myself?', or, 'What if I have a negative image of myself?' It is necessary to get rid of negative influences, judgments, and opinions that are hurtful and not true; they only exist because we allow them into our mind. No one can hurt us unless we choose to let them. The negative words (from others or ourselves) can only cause damage when we accept them as true. However, if we affirm that we are not touched or affected by them, that we reject them, and that we replace them with thoughts of love, they will not affect us. At the root of everything, there is love.

G_d, the Creator, is a loving G_d. We are not on this earth to experience hate and to embody hatred and negativity. We are here to know and spread love; we are children of the Creator; just as parents love their children, the Creator loves us.

When we forget the truth, that G_d is within each one of us, or that we were created in the image of G_d, or that there is a spark of Universal Spirit / G_d in every soul- we are distancing ourselves from G_d's love and we, in turn, do not experience true self-love. When we do not accept ourselves, or when we are critical of ourselves (in essence, we are in fact critical of the Creator for the way he made us), we then cannot experience self-love. Self-love is the ability to see beyond the socially established norms for perfection and imperfection. We must strive to see ourselves as the perfect and loving creation of the Creator. Distance from the Creator, and from the Eternal Truth of life leads to these damaging beliefs.

We are all perfect the way we are, with our unique look, talents and purpose. We are all part of Infinite Intelligence, but differentiated and connected. We were not created to suffer, but to know love. When we ultimately reach this awareness, and the truth that we exist- not because of any accident- but as a manifestation of G_d's thought, we cannot feel anything but love. We were wanted, and the Creator created us for a purpose.

Our soul / our spiritual self already knows this intrinsic truth, but our conscious mind and our beliefs are blurred and influenced by externalities that get in the way and cloud our understanding. The next time you feel unloved, look deep inside and remember- that not only are you loved and deserve love- but you *are* love. Since G_d is love, and we are part of the Creator, hence, we are also love. We need to remind ourselves of this truth by often affirming, 'I am love', 'I deserve love', 'I love myself', and 'G_d loves me', and, 'love is my Divine right'. When we reach this understanding, we are able to attain the high-energy feeling, or frequency of love, and consequently, we are able to truly send out love, be positive, and also manifest our desires.

Disappointment and Forgiveness

Forgiveness and freedom from disappointment is crucial for our progress. The only way to find peace and to move forward on our path to being better people is by letting go of seemingly bad situations and disappointments. When people appear to have harmed us- or did not stand by us, help or encourage us, etc...- do not harbor ill feelings or disappointment toward them or life. Even when our conscious mind perceives the situation as unfair, we must look at it as a life-changing experience- a good thing, and in some instances, even as an invaluable lesson for our growth.

To forgive means to let go of the negative feelings we hold within us. Forgiving also means we do not dwell on our past or any bad experience. It does not mean weakness, but rather, the courage to move on. There is no need to stay in contact with negative people; we can distance ourselves with a peaceful heart, once we have forgiven them. Remember, that when we forgive we are healing ourselves- we feel better, stronger, and peaceful. The objective is to raise our frequency and to vibrate at a higher level, but this is not possible when we are still harboring negative emotions within us.

Take to heart the truth that the Creator wants us to experience good. This means that we ought not be hasty and judge any situation prematurely. There is no need to harbor negative thoughts or ask why a certain situation happened, or why did I have to meet so and so or experience something so painful. With time and distance, we can come to see G_d's intent as good. When we free ourselves of the negative emotions associated with our seemingly bad experiences, we are better able to accept things and not feel resentment. Often times, in retrospect we are able to see the good that came out of that situation. We can and will find peace and happiness, and consequently, become suitable mediums or vessels to receive infinite good and to manifest our desires.

The Divine and Inner Power

What I call 'my inner G_d' is to know that there is a Creator and that He is *within* each one of us. To know this, means to never forget that we are all connected to Him. Our power comes from the Creator. Everything we need or want comes from the Creator; it *already* exists in the Universe, as Universal Substance, yet undifferentiated and is available to us all. He, the Creator, is the engineer / manufacturer of anything and everything in the visible and invisible plane. Thus, He alone is best equipped to fix or repair what is 'broken' or answer our requests, since He is the one that made and created everything.

Like a parent that provides for his children, we as children of the Creator are provided for by the Creator. The Creator provided us with intelligence and capabilities to solve and co-create with Him what we so desire.

Our subconscious mind creates for us, on an individual level, but always guided and directed by the Objective Universal Mind. As part of the Divine, we are able to tap into Infinite Intelligence / Source Energy and allow the Undifferentiated Substance to bring into existence our desires. The power is within us; we need to turn *inward* and to not look elsewhere for solutions. All that we need, we possess. We should not rely on humans or outside forces to create or manifest for us. We must turn our focus to G_d within (our inner G_d) and all the power that derives from knowing that truth.

Transformation Out of Pain

Why is the need and desire to positively transform oneself, more often than not, come after experiencing, something negative- a loss, torment, pain, distress, sorrow, or a feeling of hopelessness and anguish? Often times, it is in response to being in a bad place spiritually or physically. It rarely comes as the result of feeling happy or successful. It is most unusual to find happy people questioning their happiness or success, but it is customary to find unhappy people questioning their unhappiness and lack of success.

Since happiness and success are the natural way we should be and feel, there is no need to question it. However, feeling bad, unhappy, and unfulfilled is not the way we are destined to be. It is not the intent of the Creator to hurt us; it is not the natural way, and as such, we find ourselves questioning that reality. Let us look deeper to understand this phenomenon. When we are doing well and feeling comfortable- instead of looking *inward* and *thanking* the Creator for our good experiences, we are looking outward, to others, or to ourselves, i.e., our ego, and the conditions and environment around us, for justification and reason for our success. We can often hear people say, 'I win all my cases, I am such a great lawyer, surgeon, engineer', etc..., without any thought for the Creator that imbued them with such talent, or, 'I made this', 'I am that', and so on; the only thought they entertain is for the self / the ego. Where is the gratitude? What about humility?

Furthermore, when we need or desire something, we are looking outward for solutions. In essence, we are concentrating and connecting to the material world and secondary cause; we are focusing on the outside world for answers and gratification. We are not connecting to the Creator in our daily activities. Consequently, a seeming hardship comes along to set us on the right path. At first, the individual tries to solve this hardship by himself, with the help of others, or the outside world. When he realizes that all of the externalities are unable to help him, he must weather a mental thunderstorm. He finds himself confronting something that he cannot control or solve alone, or with others; he may feel lost, confused, angry, bitter, resentful, or sad. All of these negative feelings and emotions are stirring inside of him, and consequently, he starts thinking about his life, and the 'why' this is happening to him, etc...

Spiritual growth helps us understand life's occurrences. We need to evolve and to reach a level where we feel free from anxiety to face any hardship or challenge (no one claims it is easy). It is often required to experience darkness in order to find light. Time after time, we witness some life-changing event that makes us re-think the whole meaning of existence. We eventually come to realize that the problems / hardships are not what the Creator intended when he created this world. These seeming difficulties can often mean that we are in need of a wakeup call. Perhaps, we need a lesson in humility, to let go of the ego, to learn something new, to achieve more, to receive something better, or to grow, etc... These hardships are meant to re-connect us to our Source- to G_d. When we choose to see these obstacles as something for our greater good, the Creator is there to help us and to provide us with all that we need. The obstacles cease to exist when we do not think of them as bad, but as something good.

When we choose to look outward rather than inward, we fail to include G_d in our life. Consequently, we are unable to use our inner power to manifest our desires. We are left to our own devices and the law of averages. We, therefore, must connect to the Creator in order to co-create and to experience the path of least resistance on our road to manifesting.

The moment we are no longer able to solve a hardship by looking outward is the moment that a 'switch' occurs, and most of us search for spirituality and turn to the Creator, to a Higher Power. The hardship forces us to reflect and to take a good look at our life; it enables us to find our way back to the Source from which all things come. We realize that the best and fastest solutions do not come from the outside- it is not from 'you or me', or any circumstance or secondary cause in our lives- it is the realization that it is all from the Creator. He created us to live our lives with ease and joy and to connect to Him- never forgetting Him.

When we are far from our true purpose, and so disconnected, Infinite Intelligence / G_d sends us challenges and obstacles. We can then turn to our inner GPS (G_d | Power | Solution) and make use of our G_d-given creative tools in the way He intended us to live and manifest. When we exclude the Creator from our life and choose to live a life that is ego-driven, we fail to live our true purpose. We also fail to recognize the greatness of the Creator and our own unity with that greatness. Consequently, we do not benefit from all the good we are meant to have and deserve to have.

To sum up, the real way we were meant to manifest our desires is to look to G_d *within ourselves*, as co-creators, (to be proper vessels for creation). Thus, this allows the Creator to flow *through us via* our subconscious mind. To do this, we must have faith in Universal Spirit / G_d and connect to Him through our inner power our subconscious creative mind.

G_d and the Process of Creation

What does it mean to be a co-creator with G_d? It means to have faith in and to recognize Infinite Intelligence / G_d as the Creator. If we sustain this faith in Him, He in turn, will create our desired goals through us.

Our 'inner power' means- to know, that our desire, what we need or want, already exists, and is ours to take, and can become our reality through proper training and use of our subconscious mind, i.e., our 'creative mind'. The prerequisite is to remember from where the source of this power comes and to stay connected. In practice, the goal is to stay grounded and to never try to do G_d's work. We must know our role in the process of co-creation. It is the art of keeping ourselves humble and unpretentious in the midst of the greatest accomplishments and prosperity. It is important to be *grateful* and to be *thankful* for everything in our life, including the good and the seemingly not so good.

We are prompted to turn to Infinite Intelligence for guidance and direction when issues arise. He will let us know what we are required to do in order to manifest that for which we ask. **Infinite Intelligence will give us signs and a road**

map of what we need to do- our active part in the process. Further, over time, we will no longer need these signs, since our intuition will be so heightened, we will receive clear answers and directives while co-creating. With time and practice, we will develop the capacity to intuitively identify what we need to know.

Original Beliefs

Our subconscious mind controls over ninety (90%) percent of our daily life. It works on 'autopilot'. It has been 'programmed' with all it needs to function and to co-create. As such, it does not ask our intellect for guidance to keep us breathing or to perform any physical function we need for survival. As newborns, we come into this world with an empty subconscious bank, or 'clean slate'. However, as soon as we are in contact with the outside world, and its influences, our subconscious mind starts to be imprinted and filled with suggestions. Our subconscious mind is akin to a *recording device* and a *record keeper* of all our 'recordings'. This simple analogy allows us to grasp the fact that our subconscious mind does not reason, but simply gathers and receives information sent down to it by the conscious mind. It accepts as true, whatever it is given.

As babies and young kids, we have no conscious mechanism in place to reject anything we are given. We have no tools to filter out untrue statements or hetero-suggestions that are harmful to us. The purity and innocence of young children is a perfect example of the subconscious mind behaving without limited beliefs, or with very few limited beliefs.

We all had many occasions to observe young children behaving in a manner adults would never do. The constructs of fear or limitation have not yet formed within the child's mind. This will explain why they jump, climb, touch, eat, etc..., in ways only children do with no second thought or consciousness involved. They are fearless, think, and believe they can do anything, without worry for safety, harm, pain, or lack of ability. Their subconscious memory bank is not fully 'uploaded' yet.

Many things we did as children we would not do today as 'responsible' adults. I often hear people say, 'I don't know how I was able to do these things; was I out of my mind?' No, actually you were the most in touch with your pure untainted subconscious mind and unlimited abilities. Children are able to be completely free, happy, and content with very little. They truly embody the beauty and excitement of G_d's creation. Have you ever noticed the scream of joy when a baby or toddler is shown a new animal? That kind of joy is so genuine and pure, it is contagious. Adults witnessing this energy cannot help but smile and feel that joy. When we need to remember, what it feels like to be happy, joyful or positive, we need not travel far. Take the time to watch children play and you will understand. Further, if anyone needs to elevate their frequency, feel positive and happy, the fastest and easiest technique is to 'play' like or with children.

Over time, we grew farther from our inner self (our inner child) and became more and more defined and limited by the outside world and its social beliefs. We become adults with a lot of mental luggage. Even if the intent behind the auto or hetero-suggestions were for our seeming good, i.e., for our safety and preservation, the long-term effect ends up having the opposing result. These old negative beliefs are the reason why we are unable to live full and happy lives- the life we are meant to live.

The originating aim was to save us from pain, harm and perceived danger. However, the result is a mental prison that controls our life. Instead of believing in our own abilities and capabilities, we believe in limitations and why we cannot do something; we are victims of our subconscious mind and old beliefs. In practice, these beliefs were apparently adopted with our wellbeing as the goal, but in reality they no longer express what we really think or desire. Consequently, we are not free, happy, or living out our dreams. We are full of fears and doubts and we are no longer these carefree children we once were, bursting with positive energy, and unrestrained potential.

We are living life within the comfort of what we know and perceive as safe without challenging ourselves to be more or even realizing we deserve more. The 'battered wife syndrome' ('learned helplessness' and 'psychological paralysis' is a perfect example of this unfortunate situation. Choosing the bad we know versus the potential good, i.e., the unknown. **Our life is the mirror of our beliefs and experiences.** It is a continuous circle of habits and patterns of thoughts, and consequently, a predictable and foreseeable reality. If we take a closer look at our life, we can observe periodical patterns: daily, weekly, and yearly patterns. We are going to notice repeated actions, recurrent behaviors causing repeated results. Has your life changed drastically in the last year, five years, or even ten years? My guess is, probably not.

Unless we consciously (as well as unconsciously) change these habits, nothing will change. Our thoughts and results will continue to be the same. Everyone was born with inner genius, capabilities, and power. **The concept of limitation or fear is not natural- it is impressed upon us.** We are born with inner intelligence- Divine intelligence- to know what to do in times of need or emergency. Our inner knowing is part of our inner power and our inner DNA. Our subconscious mind, *through Divine intelligence,* knows what we need or what to do when we require help and protection. It is necessary for us to go back to the Source, to the beginning, to tap into our natural resources and power, and to eliminate these social and manufactured limitations.

Nighttime and the Subconscious Mind

Our subconscious mind, through our Divine intelligence, does its best work at night while we are asleep, when our conscious mind is not working or interfering with our inner wisdom. Whenever we need to make an important decision, or solve a seemingly complex problem, we are often advised to think it over or to take our time before we decide. The French have a famous expression, *'La nuit porte conseil'*, when translated in English it means, to 'sleep on it', or a more literal translation, 'night gives advice'. On the surface, it seems like an odd thing to count on night and sleep to provide us with the best advice, but on a deeper level what it means is, that we must rely on our subconscious mind to connect us with Divine intelligence to come through for us and to provide us with the best possible answer or solution while we are sleeping.

At nighttime, while we are deep asleep, our inner power can do what it is meant to do- to give us answers and solutions to what we ask. When we ask the Universal Spirit / G_d / Infinite Intelligence for something, it will not disappoint us; it will provide us with what we need. We must be alert and wait for the answer. It will come in the form of a hunch, 'sign', dream, sixth sense, or a feeling of peaceful knowing, we need to be open and listen.

When the answer comes that is the time when we need to act or follow the path revealed to us in order to achieve our goal.

Our role is to always be alert and open to accept the answer. Once we receive an intuitive response, it is our responsibility to proceed and act accordingly and with confidence, knowing that it is the perfect course of action to attain for what we have asked. Do not let doubt or outside forces influence us, because if we do, then we would have disconnected from Source Energy and should not pursue this course of action. In practice, this means that we let our intellect, fueled by fear, be in control, and allow it to detract us from listening to our intuition.

During our waking hours, Divine intelligence through our subconscious mind is not always able to send us the messages and answers we request. The reason is because, during our waking time, our thoughts are influenced by our conscious mind, as well as our subconscious mind, and hence, we might not be able to decipher the message. That is the reason why it is preferable to ask for answers just before sleep. We are required to ask every night until we get our answer (which can come at night or during the day).

The Conflict Between the Conscious and the Subconscious Mind

Another element we must be attentive to in order to recognize and remedy why we are not manifesting what we desire is the conflict between conscious and subconscious mind. We often believe that we no longer think a certain way and we are sure we have let go of an old negative belief. However, it is possible that even if on a conscious level we changed our belief and no longer think this way, on a subconscious level that change did not occur yet. There is a real likelihood that we are, unknowingly, still harboring some limited beliefs. In practice, eliminating old unwanted beliefs does not always work as fast as we would like, and thus, our subconscious beliefs remain unchanged. To believe something on a conscious level does not automatically imply it has transferred to our subconscious mind, or in the alternative, to eliminate a belief on a conscious level does not necessarily mean it is gone from our subconscious mind.

For example, we can say on a conscious level, that we no longer believe in the limiting belief that, 'to succeed you need a university degree'. Thus, for the subconscious mind to create success, we must truly eliminate that false belief about success.

Unfortunately, it is not a given, that if we think something consciously like, 'I no longer think this way about what constitutes success', that this new belief imprinted onto our subconscious mind, and that we have eliminated it and are now free of that success block.

We often find ourselves with a conflict between our conscious mind and our subconscious mind. We are being pulled by two opposing forces (reason and emotion, intellect and heart). Intellectually, one believes in the new suggestion of success, and emotionally, one does not feel it is true; it has not yet imprinted. Since, our subconscious mind is the creative mind, or the magic wand, it will not create or bring into form something it is not impressed with, or something that is contrary to what it already believes, or has in its memory bank. Remember, that when there is a conflict between the conscious and subconscious mind, the subconscious mind will always win.

At this point, our only alternative to bring forth a transformation is to make sure our subconscious mind is impressed with our new belief. We do this by auto-suggesting this new belief repetitively for as long as it takes, along with the feeling that corresponds to this belief. In practice, this means, that in order to create this new belief, we need to think of this new desired thought constantly. If we think of something long enough and repeatedly, we will end up believing it as well as imprinting it. That is how people are able to believe their own lies. Our obligation is to guard our thoughts and feelings, to not go against or contradict each other, for e.g., having a positive thought accompanied by a negative feeling. Our old belief must change in order for our subconscious mind to change and be impressed with a new belief. We have to remember that the only language the subconscious mind responds to is, emotion and feeling. Thus, it needs to feel as true what we think about most. That it is not some whimsical desire.

Do not expect long lasting positive change, even if on a conscious level our *thoughts and talk are positive*, when, on a physical / emotional level, we are *not feeling positive*, but rather, we are still feeling anxious, sad, down, helpless, depressed, doubtful, etc... Again, what we are doing is only confusing our subconscious mind by sending out mixed messages and signals to our subconscious mind and the Universe. In order to manifest, our body and mind must be synchronized. We must be in harmony with the Eternal Truth of life in our body, mind, and soul. In the same manner that we need both body and mind to function well as balanced human beings, likewise, we need harmonious unity to function well as creative beings.

When we are just starting and beginning to apply the techniques outlined in this book, for e.g., working on replacing a negative limiting belief within our subconscious mind with a positive one, we must keep a few things in mind. It is best not to affirm something that is, at least for now, in complete opposition to what is currently impressed onto our subconscious mind, and that we have a hard time believing on the conscious level too.

For e.g., if we believe that we are sick, poor, or that it is difficult to make and acquire wealth, then for the time being do not affirm, 'I am healthy' or 'I am a millionaire'. When the subconscious mind is presented with two ideas that are in opposition to each other, it will always choose the dominant one. In this case, it will choose the idea that, 'I am sick', or, 'I am poor', that is already stored in our mind. Consequently, we feel resistance to the thought-belief that we are affirming (because in our mind we have thoughts such as, 'Who am I kidding?', or, 'This is unrealistic.', or, 'How could this work?'), thus it is actually harmful to affirm the opposing belief, because in essence what we are doing is creating more resistance, and thus *strengthening the undesired belief.* Instead, what needs to be done is to choose affirmations, at least in the beginning of the process, that will not give rise to resistance within our mind (conscious and subconscious) and that do not oppose existing limiting beliefs that reside within our subconscious mind.

For e.g., if you lack wealth and you have a strong belief that it is hard for you to acquire wealth, then a useful affirmation to employ would be, 'every day I am becoming wealthier', or, 'my income is growing'; for health you would say, 'I am healing', or, 'every day I feel better', or, 'my health is improving', etc...

The idea is to affirm things that will not create any resistance or disbelief, and thus force our subconscious mind to choose between two opposing beliefs. By affirming a new belief that is neutral and non-contradictory to our subconscious mind, we are imprinting it without resistance, because it is not facing any opposing beliefs that we have deep within our subconscious mind. Additionally, our subconscious mind will not have to choose one belief over another because our new thought-belief does not threaten or contradict our old limited belief.

In essence, what we are doing is *fooling* the subconscious mind in order to imprint it with a new belief without resistance, and thus, replacing the opposing negative one. Once we affirm our non-opposing ideas long enough, with repetition and consistency, it will eventually erode the limiting belief, whereby the 'new' positive belief will be the dominant belief. In reality, we will feel a change within us and sense the truth of what we are saying. Once this happens, we can then use the stronger affirmations to impress our subconscious mind, employing affirmations like, 'I am healthy', or, 'I am wealthy', and this time they will not be rejected, but accepted, and that is when the magic happens!

Physical Demeanor

Our physical demeanor is also an indicator of how we feel. A person that does not physically stand up straight, but rather with their head down, bent forward and shoulders rolled inward, is expressing how contracted and bad they feel. The low vibrational frequency and negative feelings one exhibits physically is not the way nature and life wants us to be. That physical contraction is tied to a negative emotion that is not lifeward moving and expanding. It prevents us from self-development and growth. That physical demeanor is an outward expression of an inward feeling linked to limited beliefs within us.

On the opposite end, we have a person that stands tall, head high, not crossing arms, legs or clinching fists or fingers. That confident posture means they are open to receive Source Energy and positivity. We must not close our self from receiving blessings and good things by physically and mentally blocking the flow of good energy towards us. By physically changing our posture, we send a message to our mind, that we feel good and confident. Even if we exhibit a positive and confident posture when we do not really feel this way inside, it still has a positive impact on ourselves. It tells the world and our mind we no longer want to feel like our old self and that we are embracing a new attitude of confidence and a positive self-image. We are opening up to new opportunities and paving the way to new positive emotions.

Our mind is influenced and impressed by everything it comes across. Our physical, as well as our emotional state also have a part in affecting our mind. From an early age, our family (parents, grandparents, relatives), and later our friends, teachers, neighbors, strangers, television, music, radio, newspapers, books, movies, advertisements, religion, politics, etc..., play a big role in what we believe (or not) as adults.

Sadly, we are not educated to believe that we are extraordinary beings, and that we have many capacities and abilities to be and achieve anything we want. Our inner genius is kept hidden and unexplored. We are taught conformity and accepted social beliefs and ordinary ways. We place more importance on problems, not on solutions- on what we cannot do, rather than what we can do- on why it is impossible rather than possible. Therefore, it is no big surprise that negative feelings of fear, doubt, worry, anxiety, are the outcome. Our subconscious mind, being impersonal and having no intellectual capacity to differentiate between good or bad, cannot determine whether something is no longer true, beneficial to us, hurtful or wanted. That is why it is important for us to be aware of what we believe (or no longer believe). We need to take charge of our thought-process, and give attention to what we think about most. We must rectify, adopt, or maintain, a happy stress-free attitude and feeling, because this is what our subconscious mind requires, understands, and responds to.

When we recurrently think about a thought-desire with emotion, our subconscious mind will take that thought and compare it to the beliefs it already has in its storehouse regarding that thought-desire. Thus, habitual thoughts of worry, guilt, insecurity, unrest, anger, blame, bitterness, envy, remorse, resentfulness, or confusion will result in a reality that mirrors these feelings by manifesting itself in the outward form of disease, financial difficulties, unhappiness, low self- esteem and loss of confidence, etc...

Our mind / body is a sophisticated *intelligent machine* that is able to read our thoughts and feelings. The cells within our body are affected by our thoughts, feelings, and beliefs. Our physical health is dependent on how we direct our thoughts. Positive thoughts produce healthy cells and a healthy mind / body, and conversely, negative thoughts produce unhealthy cells, a weakened immune system and an unhealthy mind / body.

The subconscious mind is a bridge between our thoughts and our reality, between the invisible and the visible. It is also the link between our soul and the Creator. If we were to use one word to summarize the subconscious mind's driving force, the word, '*feeling*' would be best suited. **If our subconscious mind, feels as 'true', what we are saying or asking it to do, it will manifest for us, as long as we are able to sustain our *focus and will* on that desire.** But, if our feeling or emotion is not in accordance with what we are asking, our subconscious mind will not go along with our request, since the link, i.e., feeling that corresponds to it, is unavailable.

So, how do we tap into our subconscious mind to do or create the things we ask? One needs to connect to the Creator, through his subconscious mind, in order to use his inner power to co-create. When we need something, we connect to G_d and to His Infinite Powers by looking inward. By affirming with faith our connection to the Source of Everything, we put into motion our inner power. Say something like this: 'Infinite Wisdom is providing me with the answer / solution I need to solve my problem [state the problem here]. I am

Divinely directed in the steps I must follow. I am blessed to succeed. I always keep in mind that G_d supplies me with all that I need, I am thankful to Infinite Intelligence and I express my heartfelt gratitude for His infinite kindness and love'.

To sum up, our inner power is our ability to connect and to use our subconscious mind to bring forth what we want / desire. In order to do that, our conscious mind (intellect) must truly want this desire and must trust and believe in the process to manifest it. Additionally, our subconscious mind needs to *feel* the *sincerity* of our desire. Otherwise, we will have a conflict within our mind (between desire and attached emotion) and the subconscious mind will not bring into physical reality that which we half-heartedly desire.

"When an object or purpose is clearly held in thought, its precipitation, in tangible and visible form, is merrily a question of time. The vision always precedes, and itself determines the realization."

-Lilian Whiting

Part Three
My Inner Solution

There are many ways to influence, suggest or impress our subconscious mind to accept new beliefs or change old unwanted ones. Each one of us must find the practice or technique that is best suited for him. The method we choose should feel natural and easy. We can stick to one or try all methods before making up our mind as to which technique(s) works best for us.

Any method we use to impress our subconscious mind must not feel like hard work or strain us in any way. It must feel good and effortless. Our search for change and growth is not something limited by time; do not think of it as arduous, that once it is done we no longer need to do it anymore. Look at the practice as a new way of life. A continuous process, a fresh habit to keep us grounded and living a good and meaningful existence. In the same manner that people wash everyday to keep their bodies clean, so too the necessity to shower our mind with positive thoughts on a daily basis to keep it clean from negativity and destructive emotions.

If our plan is to only manifest something once and then stop, or if our goal is for something material and superficial that does not encompass some spiritual growth, we have missed the whole point of mind science. Further, we will not be able to sustain our new reality since we did not really grasp its fundamentals. Therefore, when the goal is to manifest a physical thing, without any introspection on *why* this process works, it will not sustain itself, and in essence, we did not truly understand the process of co-creating. Because, if we did, **our focus** would no longer be solely about acquiring material things (the idea is to prioritize), but rather, to have a deep appreciation for our life's purpose and our connection to the Source of everything. The order of our priorities thus becomes different. Universal Spirit knows our thoughts and our genuine motives. So, even if things might seem to work for a while, they will not uphold, unless we proceed the way the process is meant to work. To manifest our desires properly, we must embrace the Eternal Truth of life as our guideline to living a meaningful life.

We must continue and constantly endeavor to become better people than we were the day before. Personal development is a mental prerequisite. Similar to the analogy of keeping our physical bodies clean, a commitment to maintain our mind clean and positive on a daily basis is also required. We need to recognize that in order to uphold this new and better us; this process requires our daily involvement.

Techniques to Impress Our Subconscious Mind

Here is a list of the most prevalent techniques available to bring forth solutions and changes to our subconscious beliefs. An in-depth explanation for each technique with examples follows.

Affirmations

Affirmations, or autosuggestions, are a very common and simple technique we can all use to bring about our desired transformation. This is done when we speak or listen to affirmations, which are positive statements of our desires, thus recognizing the value and power of the spoken words. It is clear that words are powerful; they are the outer expression of our inner thoughts. Hence, once we utter a word, we are letting our thought speak. We are giving a voice to a thought. Therefore, our thoughts create our reality. When we say something as innocent as, 'I am not sure I can do this', we are sending a message of 'doubt' to the Universe and our subconscious mind, telling them we are unable to do this, and consequently, it will find realities and situations to match our negative affirmation. Therefore, the goal is to always concentrate on speaking positive affirmations.

Visualization

Visualization is a widespread technique that is also very efficient. The method of visualizing is to first see the thing we desire in our mind / imagination before we have actual possession of it in the physical form. It is to imagine in detail the thing we want to manifest; it is 'constructive imagination' when used to create a desired reality.

Act 'As If'

Another easy technique is to act 'as if'. This practice involves acting, behaving, and talking as if we are already in possession of the thing we desire.

Vision Boards

The technique to create vision boards or scrapbooks by assembling pictures of what we want to manifest, is known to produce good results in imprinting the subconscious mind with images of the things we desire.

Subliminal Messages

We can listen to subliminal music with messages of what we are seeking to manifest, or we can watch movies or clips of images of what we desire. Over time, we can imprint our subconscious mind.

In addition to doing any one technique, it is very important to guard our thoughts / mind from destructive influences. We must keep working and striving to improve ourselves to become truly positive and happy people. We also need to train our mind to concentrate on what we wish to manifest. Our habitual thoughts should be of gratitude for what we have, always thinking from a place of the Eternal Truth of abundance. We must let go of old ways and habits, not focusing on negativity, fear, lack, and limitation. The ultimate goal we must aspire to is to keep our thoughts positive and clean. We should do away with criticism, negativity, blame, jealousy, hate, anger, resentment, worry, and instead embrace thoughts of love, peace, health, wealth, abundance, prosperity, kindness, freedom, happiness, compassion, etc...

At first, it takes some work to teach our mind and to train our thoughts to be positive. Our mind was left to its own device for a very long time. Our habitual way has been to place more attention on the negative side of things rather than on their positive. The goal is not to see this process as some way to become holy or righteous, but to be a positive and decent human being at the outset and not at some point later on.

As such, patience and persistence is required to overcome a lifetime of (bad) habits, doubts, and insecurities. **The main reason most people do not succeed in this process is simply due to mental laziness.** They do not stick to doing what it takes to bring about the desired change. People want instant results, and refuse to give the process the time it needs. Countless amounts of people have started with good intentions, but few truly achieved their goals. To understand the process is one thing but to apply it with will and perseverance is another thing altogether. Our lack of persistence is why we fail to manifest our desires.

With time and practice, it becomes easier to stop old habits and chase away negative harmful thoughts. However, if we do not invest the needed time for the process to work, nothing will change and our old habitual ways will win. Do not let anyone fool you into believing that you can achieve anything without working at it; it takes work, and if you do not do the work, then don't be surprised when you do not get the results. A lifetime of habits is not going to change in a few minutes or couple of days' work. Dedicating a few weeks, even months, to develop new habits is not too much time to invest in order to reap such amazing results and to create new patterns that will lead us to a better life.

Affirmations and Autosuggestions in Depth

Affirmations / autosuggestions are a great way to impress our mind with new thoughts and ideas. Positive affirmations are the positive beliefs we state to ourselves. Autosuggestions are what we speak or listen to over and over in order to 'brainwash' our mind with the intent to bring forth new thought patterns and thinking habits. *Repetition is crucial*, hence, we have to listen and speak these affirmations often and every day. We need to make affirmations a part of our regular activity, for e.g., in the morning and before going to sleep. The easiest way to create new habits is by constant and regular repetition of them. **Thus, the best method is to repeat positive constructive affirmations until our subconscious mind has no alternative but to accept them as new truths.** The idea is to use suggestions in which we believe. At first, if we are not sure we believe in what we are saying, (but would like to believe it) we must then say these affirmations with *emotion and desire*, because, with enough repetition and focus, we will believe. The goal is to say the positive affirmations over and over, *even when at first we do not believe.*

If we are not sure which affirmations to say, then it is a good idea to make a list of what we want to manifest in our new reality, and then write affirmations that match. We need to listen to or make statements that support our new thoughts, in order to impress our subconscious mind and create new beliefs. The idea is to write affirmations for each desire. For example, if we want to manifest financial freedom, we can say, 'I have more money than I need', 'I am rich', 'I have enough money to live well and even more to help others', 'financial freedom is great', 'money is easy to come by', 'money wants me', or, 'I am a money magnet', etc... If you desire healing, you can say, 'I am feeling good; I am healthy and all my organs are in perfect order', 'I am healed', 'I am healing', or, 'my body is perfectly healthy'. If you want to change jobs, you could say, 'I have a great new job that I love', or, 'my new job is amazing'. When looking for love say, 'I found my soul mate', or, 'love feels great', 'I am in love', or, 'love is seeking me', etc...

Affirmations / autosuggestions must always be spoken in the *present tense*. Our subconscious mind only understands the present. What we are speaking and thinking now, at this moment, is creating our future. Thus, what we said in the past created our present reality. In practice, **from a creative 'mind science' perspective, our present reality is**

already considered our past, and does not serve our future goals or reality. However, a desire, (for the future) expressed and spoken in the present tense, sets it (the desire) in creative motion. As such, to affirm things that are negative concerning our present reality will only create more of the same reality for our future. Since words spoken in the present create the future, avoid speaking negatively about our current state of affairs. It is not a simple task to avoid speaking of the apparent reality and to actually say the contrary to what is 'seemingly' real, all with the intent to create a positive future. The goal is to keep our primary cause / goal in mind in order to create our desired future and to simultaneously stop focusing on the present as well as the past. For example, if we have debts and are unable to pay our bills, we should not say, 'I have lots of debts', 'I am in debt', or, 'I don't have money to pay my bills', even if it is just stating the seeming reality. We must understand this point well in order to ensure a good outcome. Because, if we speak of our present reality in terms of what we see or what it seems, the only thing we are doing is creating more of that same reality, or maintaining that reality with no improvement.

To change the future and to circumvent living over the same reality, we must talk and think of what we want or desire to manifest in the future, but to express it (speak it) in the present tense, as already having it or living it. It might seem intricate, but it is the only way to advance and leave lack and negativity behind.

The idea is to focus on what we do want, not what we do not want. If it were a simple process then everyone would be living in bliss manifesting his or her hearts' desire. The process is designed this way on purpose- for us to search, to find, to apply and to grow, and ultimately to reap. So again, what we are required to say is, 'I am financially free and secure', (not, 'one day I *will* be financially free'), 'I am paying all of my bills with ease', 'I have lots of money', 'I am wealthy', 'I am the best salesman in my company', 'my boss appreciates me and I am very well compensated', *even if our apparent reality does not reflect what we are saying.* Keep in mind that we are not concentrating on our present circumstance, but on the future reality, we desire to create.

If we are lonely, single and or looking for love, we cannot complain and say, 'I am not finding anyone', 'it is hard to find someone good', 'I can't find true love', 'I am so alone', or, 'my life sucks', but instead, we must overlook our present situation and *affirm with confidence and expectancy*, 'I found love' (not, 'someday I *might* fall in love'), or, 'I met my perfect match', 'I found my soul mate', 'there are many good people to meet', or, 'I am in a good relationship', etc... To reiterate, we are expressing our future reality in the present tense, and hence, are putting into motion the process that creates that reality.

If you are sick or something is hurting you, do not focus on the illness or what you have by affirming, 'I am sick', or, 'I have such and such'. Instead, concentrate on the solution and your desired goal to be healthy, rather than to affirm your unwanted condition, i.e., sickness. Thus, you would state, 'I am in perfect health', 'my body is well and I am feeling good', 'health is mine', 'I feel great', 'I am healthy, my organs and all my cells are in good health and functioning well', or, 'Infinite Intelligence / the Creator of my body is healing me and making me completely well and in perfect health', or, 'G_d within me heals me, makes me whole, and restores my body'.

We must fight the urge to speak of our negative apparent reality (not always easy but a must and becomes much easier with practice) and concentrate solely on the reality we want to bring forth. Think of it as playing a game or acting, and the only way to win or succeed is to express ourselves in the present tense while thinking of the future.

I also recommend making a list of all the old limiting beliefs we are aware of and that we wish to eliminate from our subconscious mind. To find out what limiting beliefs we need to remove, we must ask ourselves some serious questions. What is it that is blocking our progress or holding us back? What is in our past that is stopping us from moving on? What do we dislike about our reality? What are we afraid of? Alternatively, what is it that we want to manifest in our reality? What beliefs do we hold about love, health, money, success, etc...? With serious introspection and understanding, we uncover the reason why we hold such limiting beliefs and why we are not manifesting our desires, and more importantly, why we are incapable of following the natural path, of love, health, peace, abundance or anything else we desire.

This soul-searching process will result with us finding out what beliefs or habits we need to work on eliminating. This will also allow us to know what to write and to say in our new positive affirmations. It is much easier to write these personal affirmations and create new beliefs, as well as abolishing the unwanted ones, after we have done the work of digging deep within ourselves and facing what we need to change. Once we achieve this, we are able to compose some case-specific autosuggestions and affirmations for our desired life.

Further, when we write our affirmations, we need to make sure to write them by describing what we want rather than what we don't want, thus expressing our positive desire instead of stating them in the negative. For example, 'I am healthy', rather than, 'I am not sick', 'I am at my ideal weight', rather than, 'I am not overweight', 'I am rich', rather than, 'I am not poor', 'I am courageous', rather than, 'I am not afraid', and so on.

Further, we should try as much as possible to keep away from people who make negative hetero-suggestions around us. It is not always simple to avoid the negative people around us, as they can be close family members or friends. In these instances, we must make a conscious effort to reject the suggestions we are hearing, or are exposed to, by affirming to ourselves that we reject them. We can say something like, 'I do not agree with this negative belief', 'I do not share this opinion', 'this is not the way I think or believe', or, 'I reject this negative affirmation; it does not represent my view', etc...

The best time to do our affirmations is when we are in a calm and relaxed state, usually upon falling asleep and upon awakening. The reason is, that just before falling asleep, and as we are waking up, (early morning) our conscious mind is less active and thus, allows our subconscious mind to be receptive to our suggestions, without interference from our control-driven conscious mind, i.e., intellect. In addition, we can schedule more time during our day to say these affirmations. Each affirmation should last about five minutes. The practice should be easy and unforced; we do not try to coerce the imprint of these affirmations on the subconscious mind, it will only harm us. We should say our affirmations with confidence and a feeling of certitude that they are true.

The way our subconscious mind was, and still is, impressed (with negative or positive beliefs) is, *via* auto (self) or hetero-suggestions- affirmations by others- i.e., parents, relatives, friends, media, etc... In order to change these injurious beliefs, we take on positive autosuggestions that we repeat to ourselves, a few minutes several times each day. It is by creating new habits that the old impressions in our subconscious mind will be supplanted.

The notable thing to remember when practicing affirmations / autosuggestions is that the focus is placed on impressing our subconscious mind, and not on the *belief itself*.

The objective is to concentrate on the way the subconscious mind works. We must impress it until it accepts the new belief. Have faith in the power of our mind to bring about the solution we need to co-create what we desire. Thus, the important point is to get our subconscious mind to believe in our desire, rather than focusing on the desire itself (as stated before, say your affirmations even if you do not yet believe in what you are saying).

In order to help the process of imprinting our subconscious mind, it is a good idea to start paying attention to other influencing factors. It is crucial for us to guard our mind, eyes and ears. The things we read, our choice of books, magazines, and newspapers, TV shows, movies, advertisements, and news programs, should all be positive and good. Keep away from gossip, jealousy, harsh language, violence, revenge, etc... These choices may seem harmless, but they affect the soil in which our thought-seeds are germinating.

Choosing to watch things that are not full of negative messages is crucial in protecting our mind. The things we listen to are also important. Thus avoiding violent lyrics and opting to listen to words of peace, love, and harmony makes a difference to the health of our subconscious mind. When we are cautious in this manner, we are giving rise to an environment that is fertile and ready to create positivity and good vibrations.

Another element we must bear in mind is the importance of safeguarding our mind while we are sleeping. For this reason, we are required to make sure not to leave our TV, radio, and music running randomly all night long. We are not to expose our subconscious mind to hours of negative material.

The damage and exposure while we are sleeping is great, given the fact that our subconscious mind is the only one listening. Our subconscious mind never sleeps; it works 24 hours a day, every day of the week. As such, we must be smart and make the most of this valuable time. We must treat that time as a gift that assists us in impressing our subconscious mind. Another notable element to bear in mind while doing affirmations is the feeling they invoke within us when we say and hear them. Thus, it is crucial for us to feel good when we say them. One simple way to raise our vibration is to include background music or singing while doing our affirmations. There are a great number of affirmations in song format available on CDs, YouTube or on the internet at large. We can also listen to music we enjoy as we say them. The idea is to match a good sensation / feeling to our affirmations. Thus, any method we can think of is good, as long as it raises our vibration.

As said previously, 'words have power'. The famous words, '*Abra*' '*Cadabra*', conjure the idea of bringing something into the visible from the invisible. They have their root in mind science. In the Hebrew language, the word, '*Abra*', means 'to create', and the word, '*Cadabra*', means, 'as spoken'. Consequently, **we create with words**. Hence, it is imperative to choose our words carefully at all times, because our words create our reality. To go back one step, we must remember that before we speak these words, they were thoughts in our mind. Therefore, not only do we have to guard our speech, we first must cultivate good thoughts.

Visualization in Depth

The practice of visualization is another prevalent and easy method used to impress our subconscious mind to manifest our desires. This technique is simple as well as enjoyable. We can practice visualization by closing our eyes and seeing in our mind the object of our desire already in our possession. This means that we see ourselves as already having it, living it, and feeling it. With this technique, we employ all of our physical senses to experience in our mind the object of our desire.

Visualization is the use of imagination in the process of creation. There are two ways to use imagination, the constructive or destructive way. Thus, one must make a conscious choice to use his imagination constructively.

The smell of the ocean, walking on the beach with our soul mate, hosting a party in our new house, or seeing the doctor telling us that we are healed, etc..., are examples of feel-good visuals that we can experience in our mind. For visualization to be most effective, we should not force ourselves to visualize. The exercise should be fun to do and most pleasing, since it is, after all, seeing the things we desire most. If we are struggling with visualizing or imagining something new or unknown to us, we must stop trying to compel visualization, and instead, start with a simpler procedure. Start with thinking of something that is easier to imagine- something familiar or similar to the one we desire- and start visualizing ourselves having it. For example, if we want a beach house for family vacations, we can find a picture of a beautiful house that depicts our liking and style and visualize something similar as being ours. Over time, it will become easier for us to add personal details to the images in our mind. In order to stir positive emotions while visualizing, ask yourself *prior* to visualizing, 'what would it be like if [insert your desire here] was realized right now?' This will give you a positive feeling **in the present moment** now- that the desire is already here- a necessary step to manifesting. Remember, the subconscious mind only reads emotions, it works in real time (not past or future), and is the 'engine' of creating.

An important fact to remember is not to covet something someone else has. We can desire and visualize a similar style house but not express, 'I want the house of so and so' (unless it is for sale). Or, when we want to meet someone, we should never request from G_d / Infinite Intelligence for a specific person, or to meet someone that is already in a relationship (similarly, we would not want anyone to take what is ours). The idea is to ask for and visualize what is rightfully ours, destined for us by Divine plan, in a positive manner without infringing or hurting anyone in the process.

For visualization to work well we must include many details, as well as, include ourselves in the mental images we are visualizing. We are also encouraged to take part in the visualization of our desire. Doing this has an even superior impact on our subconscious mind. For example, when we visualize our new beach house, it is nice to include all of the details- furniture we like, colors, accessories, layout, size- but even more powerful is seeing ourselves sleeping in that new home, cooking in our new kitchen, playing in the garden, looking at the view from our terrace, etc... The more involved we are in our visualization, the better.

Our visualization should be done in a quiet place where we can have the peace of mind to visualize without interruption or noise. We can visualize at home, in our car, at work, or in the park outside. It is a good idea to try to have as many sessions per day, or at least two to three visualization sessions per day. These sessions do not need to be long, but a few minutes each time is sufficient.

If possible, aim to have one short visualization session before going to sleep. Visualizing before sleep has many benefits. We are making sure that the last images in our mind, before we drift off to sleep, are of the things that we love and desire. Furthermore, the last feelings we have will be of happiness and contentment in seeing them. Visualizing the outcome is very powerful for imprinting the subconscious mind right before sleep.

These positive feelings and images before sleep are going to stay with us all night, since they were the last thoughts and images in our mind. The benefits are not only good on our inner self, but also on our outer self. In the morning, when we wake up after a night filled with positive thoughts and pleasant images, we feel energized, happy, and positive. As opposed to waking up, tired and in a negative mood after a night of negative thoughts, images and feelings. In view of the fact that our first emotions upon waking reflect the feelings, we had prior to sleep, it is crucial to guard our thoughts just prior to sleep. Never go to sleep upset, angry, crying, thinking of and rehashing all the negative events of that day. Always go to sleep with positive thoughts of happy things and of our desired reality.

We must keep our subconscious mind clean and away from harmful influences. It is not only an excellent way to impress our subconscious mind, but also a great beginning for our transformation in becoming positive people. Once we start making small changes daily in our thoughts, speech and acts, we will notice qualitative differences in ourselves. For example, the transformation will be in the way we feel, speak, and think. The manner we project ourselves physically, our demeanor and the way people talk and react to us, will also change. The transformation is subtle at first, but over time people will start to notice, remarking that we look different, we sound different, we act different, more at ease, happier, smiling, and in actual truth, we are different. This new 'me' feels so good that it motivates 'me' to continue on this path of self-development and spiritual growth.

We must make sure to visualize often and consistently. Always visualize the same thing or something very close to our desire. The idea is not to confuse our subconscious mind, or even worse, send it conflicting messages. We need to be clear and precise with what we ask for and with the images and visuals we have in our mind. For example, do not visualize a new job one day, a city apartment the next day and a vacation the third day. We should make sure to be consistent and focus on our goal in an orderly manner.

Always visualize with a sense of great calm and joy, having faith that our desire will materialize. Having faith in the Creator is enough to ensure a sense of peace and certainty in knowing that we will receive what we desire. Never try to figure out how it will come to us, or try to map out the mechanics of it, or whether it is possible or even realistic.

If any of these thoughts enter our mind, we are disconnecting from the creative powers at work. Our contribution to the process is to know what we want, to know that we are getting it, and to express gratitude before having it, never questioning 'how and when' it will happen. There is no place for doubt and fear if we are truly at peace. Whatever we undertake to do or co-create, we have to keep the Creator in our mind, and thus feel calm and harmonious.

Meditation

The practice of meditation is very beneficial when we want to get in touch with our inner self. Meditation is very helpful in clearing our mind, quieting it and letting it be at rest. Meditation is also a great way to still our mind and connect to Source Energy. While meditating, we are letting go for a little while of the outside world and we are concentrating on our inner being. We must make a daily point to **connect our thoughts to the Creator as the Source of everything**. Meditating and focusing on the Source of everything, in our life and in the Universal Plane, will always keep us grounded and connected to Infinite Intelligence and to our power to co-create.

Since the Creator is infinite, He is not limited in time and in space. As such, He is everywhere at all times. This means that the Creator is in me at all times, and therefore, He is in my subconscious creative mind at all times. For that reason, my power to co-create is infinite and is not bound by time and space. Meditating and becoming calm strengthens the union of our individual power to the Universal Power. Meditation sustains our bond to Source Energy of creation and to our subconscious mind that creates for us. Hence, to include meditation in our daily routine is recommended. We should take as little as five minutes (optimum about 30 minutes) each day to meditate and we will appreciate the many benefits that ensue.

Some people meditate while listening to binaural beats- specific sound frequencies that affect or induce a particular brainwave in our mind associated with certain feelings or states of consciousness. Some of the pertinent brainwaves that are induced with binaural beats technology are:

⇒ Gamma (>40 Hz)- these waves assist in mental activity, problem-solving, consciousness, fear

⇒ Beta (13-25 Hz)- enhances thinking, focus, stress release

⇒ Alpha (7-13 Hz)- increases relaxed focus

⇒ Theta (4-7 Hz)- deep relaxation, sleep, reaching the subconscious

⇒ Delta (<4 Hz)- very deep sleep

Mediation can be enhanced while experiencing a particular brainwave-state. When experiencing such a state, we can feel as though we are under hypnosis, which allows the subconscious mind to be more amenable to suggestion. For most people, using binaural beats is safe, however, for certain medical conditions, pregnant women and children, it is not recommended. Before using binaural beats, it is recommended to read about it, and if you have a medical condition, please consult your physician.

Breathing Exercises

To practice concentrated breathing is an excellent way to strengthen ourselves and to find inner peace and calmness. Taking deep breaths (through our nose and / or our mouth) and then slowly exhaling (through our nose and / or our mouth) is a prompt way to fight fear, panic, or anxiety and to connect to our inner self. We must make the time, every day, to perform this simple technique that instantaneously makes us feel better. A few minutes are all it takes. Further, to practice concentrated breathing keeps us in the present moment. It is a great way to allow our mind to rest and to be peaceful, in order to manifest our desires.

Vision Board and Scrapbook in Depth

Another fun way to induce our subconscious mind to accept new beliefs and to get rid of old ones is to create a vision board or a vision scrapbook. By looking at images and choosing ones we love and desire, we help the impression process of our subconscious mind. We are required to fill our board or book with many images that we want manifested, and that in turn, will create in us a sense of satisfaction and joy, in expecting them. We should keep our board or book near us, where we can look at it daily, particularly in the morning, and before sleep. The object is that every time we look at our board or book, it sends our subconscious mind messages and images of what we want, believe, and feel. Looking at the board is a feel-good trigger that reminds our mind of our goals and desires.

Our mind stores every image on our board or book in its memory bank; it now knows what we desire. We must make sure that our habitual thoughts, behavior and words do not contradict, or put into question, the likelihood of obtaining our heart's desire, because a conflicting behavior will only delay or destroy our creative process. Our vision board or book does not need to be filled in one day; we can add new images and sayings to the board or book on an ongoing basis. The idea is to enjoy the making of this board or book, since it represents what we love, our dreams and goals. Enjoy the activity of putting it together, and the pleasure and happy feelings it brings when we look at it.

To 'Act As If' in Depth

Another method that can be used to affect our subconscious mind is, to 'act as if *we are already in possession* or living our desired life. 'Acting as if' means we are pretending and believing we already are, or have, what we asked for. Play the part, dress the part, talk the part, etc... For example, if we want to start our own business, talk like a businessperson, think like a boss- dress the part. If people ask us what we do for a living, we can present ourselves as a businessperson, etc...

If we want to travel, we can prepare a suitcase and have it ready; we can even go to the airport and get the sense, feeling, and excitement of travelers. We can pretend we are already there at our dream destination. We can eat foods similar to the ones found in that country, such as eating Italian food, if we want to travel to Italy. Never think of lack, or what we do not have. Concentrate on being positive and happy. Be sure of the outcome, that we are healthy, that the vacation we desire is ours, that we are getting married, that we find a great job, that we have all the money we need and more, etc... Never question the result. Keeping our faith and expectancy are the key to success.

Subliminal Messages in Depth

To listen to or to watch subliminal messages is a technique that targets our subconscious mind. The idea is to use specific words, messages, sounds, and images that are expressed rapidly and in a hidden way, with the intent to imprint our subconscious mind. Most often, our conscious mind is not able to see and hear these messages, because the target is the subconscious mind. Thus, listening to subliminal music or watching subliminal videos is helpful in impressing our subconscious mind.

Similar to the techniques described above, the strategy is for us to create a sense and feeling of positive energy that will match our desires. Hence, watching images and / or listening to subliminal music that we enjoy and that depicts our desires, will result with our subconscious mind recording and storing these messages in our memory bank. This practice with time and persistence can lead to a change in our beliefs. However, one must be realistic in his practice of listening and watching subliminal messages. Do not naively expect a total metamorphosis after a few hours of listening or watching them. Keep in mind, when doing any one technique; we are working to bring change to a lifetime of old beliefs and patterns. Perseverance and patience are a prerequisite. Any technique we choose to use consistently and diligently in seeking self-development is going to help us unlearn what took years to learn. Therefore, when we practice any one technique, we must remember that it took many years to accumulate these negative habits and beliefs, and thus, it will take some time in getting rid of them.

When we are experiencing trouble in eliminating a destructive and harmful belief, do not despair and do not give up. We must take that belief, the one we are struggling with, and are unsuccessful in replacing, and simply speak to Infinite Intelligence of our difficulty. Once we openly express our desire to get rid of this belief, as well as, our difficulty in doing so, then, we turn it over to the Universe, by asking for help and solutions. Say something like, 'I acknowledge that I am having a hard time letting go of this limited belief [insert the belief...] and I ask Infinite Intelligence / G_d within me to guide and help me remove this belief in the best and fastest way'. The whole act of 'releasing the belief' will bring forth solutions for removing it from our subconscious mind. Sometimes, the simple act of releasing it to the Universe does the job of eliminating it. In the interim, we should not stop practicing our chosen technique, for positive imprinting of our subconscious mind.

Choice of the Company We Keep

Anything we can do to help create a positive 'me' will in turn help create a positive 'reality'. Thus, our choice of company can also play a role. If we are always surrounded with people that are negative, complain, criticize, gossip, and that only see problems and never see solutions, we are in danger of being negatively affected. The energy of these people is very low and unproductive, and as such, they are not helping us grow or expand into better people. Furthermore, bad company hampers our progress and can delay our improvement. Therefore, we need to choose wisely with whom we spend a lot of time. We cannot choose our family, but we have a choice when it comes to friends. Like the famous saying, 'Tell me who your friends are and I will tell you who you are'; if we are surrounded by positive kind people there is a greater chance that we are also positive and kind. Choose wisely; it is after all a reflection of 'you'.

Walking

The practice of taking a walk and using that time to think of our goals is very productive, as well as efficient for raising our feel-good vibration. A daily walk of any amount of time (as little as five minutes) is beneficial for our mind. The goal is to use wisely that time while we are walking, to think and to see our desires as realized. It is also a good time to say and to listen to affirmations. Walking is an excellent method to improve our frame of mind, to elevate it to a feel-good sensation. If you are able to walk in a park, forest or on a mountain, it is even more beneficial; the energy of nature and trees is calming, peaceful, and favorable for our growth and for attaining the required mental attitude needed for manifesting. A short walk, which includes affirmations, is a great way, to kick-start our day. The idea is to set a positive tone for the day. Therefore, it is good to say something like, 'What a beautiful morning!', or, 'I know that this day is amazing, it can only be good, since Infinite Wisdom is the One that guides me in all my endeavors'.

Dancing and Singing

Another fun way to raise our vibration and our mood is to listen to pleasurable uplifting music. It often triggers good memories and makes us feel good. Some people take on the practice of singing fun tunes in their head or singing along to a favorite song. Dancing is another way to help us feel good and happy. Have you ever tried to listen to a song that you love first thing in the morning and notice how fast your mood can change? It never misses; that feel-good moment along with feeling energized. Make sure to choose a song that is upbeat and happy. If the urge to dance arises, then do it; it can only make us feel better. We will raise our energy level, feel amazing, and burn a few calories. The idea is to start the day on a high note or positive vibration. A short three-minute song / dance can lead to hours of positive energy and productivity; we should never underestimate the effect it can have on our day. If we have an exercise or activity that makes us feel good, then we can practice it in order to elevate our energy. The goal is to be happy and feel upbeat; we should choose the technique that works best for us.

Positive Talk

We must develop the habit to say positive things all day long, but especially first thing in the morning. For example, say, 'What a beautiful day, thank you G_d', or, 'I'm accomplishing a lot of good things today'. When we do this, we are setting the way for our day. In addition, it is important to adopt the habit of answering people we encounter early in the morning, with positive words, so that the Universe can bring forth an environment and reality to match our words. Next time someone asks us, 'How are you?' answer strongly, 'Amazing!', or, 'I am great.', or, 'I am doing well'. Never answer negatively or with bad feelings, even if it is the apparent truth or the way we feel at that moment. Hence, avoid saying, 'I'm not feeling well.', or, 'I'm sick.', or, 'Everything is falling apart.', or, 'I'm having a terrible day', etc...

Harmful Self-Talk

Be aware that unintended self-talk, even if done in a joking manner or in a non-serious way, can harm the process and our progress. Since our subconscious mind cannot tell the difference between when we are serious and when we are not, we must make sure to never utter words or thoughts that we do not really mean. Our subconscious mind does not know when we are kidding. Thus, never say, 'I'm such an idiot', or, 'I'm broke', or, 'I don't know', or, 'I'm sick in the head', or, 'I'm bad', etc...

Even if we do not really believe in what we are saying, over time our subconscious mind will take us literally, and bring forth a reality to match our affirmations. Be careful and make a conscious effort to not affirm thoughts that are negative, even jokingly. If we catch ourselves doing this, we must say to ourselves on the spot, 'I did not mean this', or, 'this is not what I think or believe', and then make sure to affirm something positive that we do believe in, to replace it, such as, 'I'm smart', or, 'I'm healthy', or, 'I'm doing very well', etc... The idea is to keep our mind clean of harmful thoughts. Any method that we know of which accomplishes this goal, is good, but should always be in a lifeward manner, without harming anyone in the process.

To sum up my inner solution, it is to know that nothing stands in the way of our will. As such, we need a sincere desire (with positive emotion attached) along with will and focus on that desire, until it manifests. If we do not have the indispensable positive emotion, then, we need to reach it. Using the techniques outlined in this book will help us achieve this.

"Everything can be taken from a man but...the last of the human freedoms- to choose one's attitude in any given set of circumstances."

-Viktor Frankl

Part Four
Tying It All
Together

"Everything you see has its roots in the unseen world."

-Rumi

Part Four – Tying It All Together   / 153

My Mind as a GPS

My mind is a GPS (and more accurately the GPS is like my mind); it can take me anywhere, to any desired destination, at any time, in the best and shortest way. I only need to let the GPS do what it was designed to do. My role is to input one 'destination-address' at a time. The GPS knows the way to all destinations, but it will only work when I input one desired destination at a time. Once I input a correct address, with all of the details- street name, number, city, country, zip code- the GPS does the rest. It configures the most efficient course to get me where I want to go. However, if I insert more than one destination at once, even as little as two destinations, I misuse it by not following the manufacturer's instructions. Consequently, it will not take me anywhere; it will not work, notwithstanding the fact that it knows how to reach both destinations.

Our mind works in the same manner as a GPS. It follows the instructions of the Creator. We must first give it a precise 'destination', i.e., one specific goal at a time, with details unequivocally and clearly stated, and it will get us to our destination. It knows how to get us to where we want to go in the fastest and most efficient way. Our subconscious mind has the ability to manifest all the things we can imagine, but only if we do it in an orderly fashion, one desire at a time. Do not create chaos and confusion; do not send many requests / goals at the same time. Think of one goal; be thorough and unambiguous when describing that goal. Do not mix the thought-requests. If you follow the GPS' 'operations manual', you will achieve your goal.

In practice, this means that our thought-desire cannot materialize until we do our part. Once we have a sincere thought-desire, we need to focus on that thought, and be receptive to the creative process of Infinite Intelligence in our subconscious mind. Our desire, coupled with our will, allows us to channel that thought-desire and separate it from the rest of the wandering thoughts we think about all day, every day.

Since we think about thousands of thoughts an hour it is important to differentiate our desired thought from the random undesired ones. Given the fact that we do think many thoughts, we do not want or desire to manifest all of them. The process to manifest the thought we do want requires us to do more than think that thought once. We must think that thought repeatedly until it is distinguished and differentiated from our other thoughts. It is a conscious desire that must move from the random thinking process to the creative process. Our desire must be more than just a thought we think of occasionally.

We are required to ensure that our desire is aligned with the Universal Truth of life, because the Creator does not assist us or create through us something that is in conflict with the essence of life. Any goal that goes against morality, humanity, love, peace, goodness, etc..., does not follow the laws of nature and will not get nature's assistance.

Even if sometimes it seems like some people do get things by employing negative ways, be sure that the Universe has no part in it and brings everything into balance. No good deed goes unrewarded and no bad deed goes without retribution. Do not believe in bad ways to succeed, it does not pay and will not last.

Moving from random thinking to thinking in the creative process means we are now directing and guiding our thoughts. It is no longer a haphazard wandering thought, but a desire, a thought we want, backed by our will. This, in turn, allows us to tell Infinite Intelligence with confidence what we desire. We can now have a mental image, and the Universe can form a prototype of that which we desire. We need to maintain our focus on that desire, while we ask the Creator to guide and direct us, (through our subconscious mind), on what we need to do. If we must do anything, the Universe will find a way to convey it to us.

In summary, our individual creative power is in motion when: we are thinking about our desire with emotion; when we keep our intention and will on that desire; when we maintain a high vibration / emotion / feeling on our desire up until its physical manifestation, and when we have faith and certainty in the outcome. All of this is made possible if we acknowledge the Creator as the Source of everything and connect to Him through our subconscious mind.

The Role of the Subconscious Mind

The subconscious mind responds to our thought-desire by manifesting our desire in the physical realm. It is the creative power within us. When we do not get the results we want, it means that something in the chain of creative motion did not work properly. We must then take a closer look at the process flow of creation in order to address and remedy the matter and for the creative motion to resume:

Ten Steps to Manifesting

1.　**Directed Thought** (not random)

2.　**Sincere Desire-** leading to a committed decision

3.　**Positive Emotion-** a good feeling attached to the thought / desire

4.　**Constructive Imagination-** seeing and visualizing in our mind what we want to manifest

5.　**Will-** to stay focused on the desire until it has manifested in the visible realm

6. **Prototype / Spiritually Manufactured Model**- when we keep our will on our desire, the Universe creates a spiritual replica of that desire based on the details we gave

7. **Faith in the Outcome and the Creator**- as the Source of our Supply

8. **Turning to the Subconscious Mind**- our link to the Creator. We turn over our desire to the Universe, through the channel of our subconscious mind, and patiently wait for the answers and solutions

9. **Intuitive Leads** - the Universe sends details and answers to manifest our desire, be open to receive and act

10. **The Law of Attraction starts to operate** - solutions appear, outside of our habitual realm, for example, things start to happen, ideas emerge, opportunities arise, solutions enter our mind, hunches, unexpected people comeforth, etc...

After reviewing the process flow, we can determine which step(s) we missed or did not complete. This, in turn, will allow us to make adjustments in our thoughts and behavior in order to bring us back into creative alignment.

Gratitude, Giving and Receiving

Gratitude is the mother of all virtues. It is an important practice we should never overlook or underestimate. To offer gratitude or be unconditional givers enables us to become proper vessels to receiving. I cannot stress enough how fundamental it is for our transformation. Being grateful to the Creator on a daily basis and expressing it in words, thoughts, and deeds is indispensable. We must express heartfelt gratitude for everything in our life. We need to be grateful for our desire *before* it manifests into physical form. Furthermore, we must learn to see the seemingly bad things in our reality as good, as well as, feel grateful for them. This, in turn, gives the Creator grounds to reward us with good things, for our faith and trust in Him. The progress we seek and the motivation to 'grow' comes from these apparent bad realities.

The test is to be grateful for the challenges, roadblocks, obstacles, and difficulties. It is not complicated to be grateful for anything good in our life. The real test comes during times of lack and difficulties; this is when we demonstrate our faith and belief that everything is for our good. Gratitude shines in the face of hardship. To be grateful in tough times means we see things with an inward vision of a knowing heart and not with an outward vision of our physical senses.

Similarly, to give when we do not have is a sure way to reap returns. To be unconditional givers is a great way to warrant more; the natural Law of Reciprocity rewards generosity. Never question the benefits of a good deed. Giving can be in the form of our time, our self, our money, and or our services.

We experience a positive outcome when we demonstrate that we do not question the Creator, and that we accept without reproach the seemingly bad experiences in our lives. Like a rainbow after rain, we must keep the image of our mental rainbow and be certain of its physical manifestation in order to experience it. Receiving is an important part of the process; one should not be so absorbed in giving, that he fails to see that he is entitled to receive. The Creator gives us signs of what we need to do, or follow, to attain what we desire. A job, healing, a soul mate, money, or opportunities, are seeking us, but we must be open and alert for all the good that is coming our way.

Keeping a gratitude journal is a great way to keep us connected to the Creator and Giver of everything in our life. Every day we should practice expressing our gratitude. Start with writing a few things or even one thing only. The good feelings we get as a result will motivate us to keep this practice a part of our daily routine. We can also express our gratitude verbally, if we prefer.

This technique does not have to be complicated; it can be something as simple as saying, 'thank you Infinite Intelligence for waking up, for breathing', 'thank you G_d for the beautiful morning', 'thank you Universal Spirit for the great experiences today brings', 'thank you for my health', 'thank you for my family', etc... Each day that we are fortunate to wake up, we must think, 'today is like my birthday'. If we are blessed to wake up in the morning and are still breathing, we are thus given another day to start anew and to be anything we want to be, and to do anything we wish to do. The possibilities for each day are endless, so as our unexploited potential. Be grateful for the little things they are the pathway to being grateful for the bigger things.

The Hidden Good

Most good things are first hidden from us. In order to see them and appreciate them, we must believe with faith that they exist. The way to see them manifested in our physical reality is to focus on them with will and consistency until they are realized (wave / particle duality). For most of us, our own personal abilities and potentials are hidden from us. However, (if we are sincerely searching) there will be a time when we come to realize that we are able to do and be anything that we want. This ability exists within all of us. There are more treasures in the invisible plane than there are in the visible one. Nothing can stand in the way of desire blended with faith and will. When we attain the ability to have faith, (with desire and will), we reach a harmonious mental state. Our within and without are in harmony, and consequently, we are vibrating at a high frequency that enables us to manifest as positive beings.

The simplest way to manifest and to co-create is to understand our inner GPS and its key elements. We can think of our inner GPS (G_d | Power | Solution) in this way:

G_d = Faith (when we think of G_d, we think of faith- our faith in G_d, our faith in the process and our faith in the outcome.)

Power = Desire transmitted to our subconscious mind (when we think of power we know that our desire will manifest; if we have a strong unwavering desire, then we have the power to manifest.)

Solution = Will to hold our desire in our thoughts (we know, that through our persistent thinking, i.e., will, our desire will manifest.)

$$\boxed{\text{GPS = FDW}}$$

> **Our Inner (G_d + Power + Solution) = Faith + Desire + Will**

In practice, to discover 'my inner GPS' means to have faith, desire, and will, where:

Faith is to know and to understand that the Creator is within me- my inner G_d- is to know that the Creator is infinite, and that He provides and Creates everything, seen and unseen. He is everywhere, at all times. Thus, he is within me at all times. Since I am His creation, and a part of Him, I am connected to Him, and to Infinite Supply. When I am truly able to believe this Universal Truth, then I am able to act with faith. Thus, our inner G_d means to have faith in the Creator and the outcome.

Desire is my inner power. It lets my subconscious mind know what I truly desire. It is to know with certitude that I can have or be what I want, through the medium of my creative mind (my subconscious mind). Thus, inner power, in practice, is to have a sincere desire and to know that my subconscious mind will bring it into physical reality. Since, our subconscious mind is the Life Principle (G_d) within us and is our link to the Creator; we must then ask Infinite Intelligence within us for the manifestation of our desire.

Will is my inner solution. It is to know with confidence that once I made a firm decision to have what I desire, my inner solution comes from my will. It is the constant focus and attention on my desire until it comes into the physical plane. When I keep my will on my desire, and my subconscious mind believes it as true, the Law of Attraction, the forces of nature, the Universe all work together to provide me with the solutions and answers that I need to achieve my desire. Thus, inner solution, in practice, is to apply will- a steady and constant focus on my desire with attention on my thoughts, words, and actions, until it manifests in my reality.

Consequently, the simplest equation to describe reality is thoughts plus energy:

$$\boxed{R = T + E}$$

Thoughts: are what we think and focus on most of our time. (For a wanted reality, it is thinking of our sincere desire with will unfaltering, with inner peace and faith, knowing it will manifest.)

Energy: is the emotion that our thoughts emit and our subconscious mind senses. The more positive the energy the quicker we manifest (when the energy we send out is negative, we cannot manifest a positive reality).

Trust the Process and Be Still

As mentioned previously, when we engage in the process of co-creating, we must have faith and trust in the Creator. We must let go of forcing or coercing the process. As well, in our daily life, we must show faith and trust that Infinite Intelligence will guide and direct us in all that we do. G_d is in charge; we are not the drivers, but are the co-pilots. We must learn to follow the path of least resistance and 'go with the flow'. What feels hard, or seems to resist our efforts, is probably the wrong path to reach our goal. We need to listen to and understand the signs and messages that Universal Spirit is sending us. It is crucial to pay attention to our intuition; it might seem like a hard thing to learn but when we sincerely try, we are able to reach inner knowing, to understand what we must do or not do.

When we are experiencing moments of frustration and anger, (because it appears we are not manifesting our desire), the Universe is letting us know and sending us messages that say, 'not yet', 'not right now', 'not this path', 'not that way', 'try it this way', or, 'not that thing', etc... We must train ourselves to 'listen' to the Creator, through our intuition. If we do not, then we are not connecting to Source Energy. Moreover, we are stopping the flow of creation or manifestation. The objective is to grow from life's 'lessons,' when this does not happen, we get more (similar) lessons until we do. Let go of worry, fear, doubt, stress, anxiety, and trust with peaceful certitude that we are getting what we desire. In practice, it is to know that we will succeed, get what we want, find what we are looking for, and reach our destination, without thoughts concerning conditions or feelings of anxiety. We will manifest in due time according to 'Natural Law'. **The 'how' and 'when' is not within our purview.**

Just as a tree seed planted under the earth's soil cannot be rushed and will not cut corners to grow tall and healthy, so too are our thoughts that are implanted within our subconscious mind. It follows the Natural Laws needed for its growth: fertile soil, water, sun, and the exact amount of time, but always knowing that the outcome will be a beautiful tree. Thus, the next time we are about to get upset or troubled over something not going our way, or working out the way we want, we need to stop and think to ourselves, 'I must take a step back.', or, 'What is Infinite Intelligence trying to tell me?', or, 'I need to give the process a little more time.', or, 'I'm trying too hard.', or, 'I need to stay positive', etc... We must learn to listen to our gut and our intuition; it will lead us to understand the right solution.

Do Not Speak of Your Journey

I would like to touch upon what we could expect from many people once we begin this process. When we start this amazing journey, we are not always going to get support. People will also try to dissuade us. If we speak of our goals and ideas to people, we are bound to hear negative remarks like how unrealistic, naïve or unlikely it is for us to succeed. It is not necessarily coming from a bad place, but it is surely coming from a place of not knowing, i.e., ignorance. Nonetheless, it is damaging for our process and us. Most people are not spiritual, or do not know much about mind science and metaphysics, and thus, to discuss this subject with them at the start of our journey, is not a good idea. For many people only conditions, circumstances and environment (the physical material world) matter and not anything else that exists in the invisible plane. Society follows conformity, thus, when we go outside of what people know or comprehend resistance is to be expected. However, one needs to keep in mind that most innovators, creators, movers and shakers, were forward thinkers and did not conform to social norms, but rather, challenged the *status quo*. They were not part of the majority, but rather a tiny minority. Thus, expect skepticism regarding this new way of thinking and being, it is natural. We will hear, 'How come you are not manifesting yet?', or, 'You see I told you this is nonsense!', or, 'I have not seen any improvement in your life', etc...

In order to avoid many heated conversations, in which we will have to defend ourselves, it is better not to talk about our journey until we have manifested our desire. Since people are curious and want to know what we are doing and how we are doing it, it is better for us to let our results and transformation speak for us. Thus, as a rule, resist talking about the process. To have our ideas or actions mocked or ridiculed can only delay our advancement or progress.

Further, do not try to win over people by trying to convince them or teach them how the process works. It is very detrimental for our advancement to have arguments with people who do not support our journey of self-development. People that are neither knowledgeable on the subject nor passionate about it, or are simply not at our level, will only accept tangible results and not grand theories. Therefore, we should keep the preaching and the unsolicited advice to ourselves, until the time when we have more than just words to back up what we are saying.

Expect Resistance but Stay Strong

The second thing to be aware of is, that once we start the process of manifesting, resistance from within and outside of us will come knocking. So be prepared for challenges, moments of hesitation, for wanting to abandon ship, to let go or give up. To know this in advance helps us win the struggle. Do not fall prey to this expected occurrence. To have low energy and feel overwhelmed is normal. We must keep in mind that when we begin this process, we are reversing old habits, and eliminating bad beliefs. It is the beginning of adopting new beliefs and new habits, thus, resistance will appear. Our old self is not going to give up so easily. **It's a turf war between the old us and the new us, the one that does not give in, wins.** When we 'think' that we are actually making good headway and we further, feel and see positive change in the horizon, the opposing forces show up and try to derail us with thoughts of doubt, worry, setbacks, challenges, resistance, obstacles, loss or failure, etc... We should be aware that it is actually a good thing to experience confrontation in the process. Since it is a way to know and have proof that the Universe has taken notice of the change that is happening in our life. As such, the Universe is testing us, to make sure that this change is something we genuinely want. It needs to know that we really want this and that it is not some whimsical desire. Be sure not to look at these seemingly negative appearances and to be negatively influenced by them. We should not let them detract us from our path. We must resist and keep our focus on our desired goal until it manifests. Our old self is only trying to maintain the *status quo,* since this is all it knows. It is not yet sure or aware of the truth of our new beliefs and habits. So, the more we stick to what we want, and follow the road to change, with consistency and faith, the more we will convince our old self of the sincerity of our new desires.

In order to fight these seemingly negative moments that are trying to draw us back and stop our progress, and in order for us to succeed, we need to understand what is happening to us and why we are feeling this way. Our old self (with our old beliefs and our old habits), is refusing to accept lightly, without a good fight, these new thoughts and beliefs, and the desired change that it entails. It is not familiar with these new requests, and that is the reason why it is fighting and resisting the change. Our subconscious mind is using all it has in its memory bank of feelings, emotions, and beliefs, to review our past thoughts, experiences, knowledge, influences, and actions, in order to react and oppose the new goals and beliefs that we are sending its way.

There is a transition time- an adjustment time needed for the new thoughts we are sending out into the Universe, and for the reprogramming of our subconscious mind and creative self- to become aligned and on the same page. We must be aware that we do have the ability to control this process and to stay in command of our mind. We need to say, 'I am in control of my mind, and I desire this new belief', etc... Do not become a victim of our old thought patterns and habits; they are going to resist us, and our desires, until our new ones are impressed. Our subconscious mind must feel our new beliefs as true, until this happens; we have to focus on what we are trying to achieve.

If we give up now at this point, then we are letting our old thoughts control and deprive us of what we deserve. Do not let it happen; we have a choice. We can react in one of two ways: the negative way, to be discouraged- to stop, to give in to pressure- and to stay with things the way they are. On the other hand, the positive way- to stay on course, always remembering our goals and ignoring the conditions, circumstances and obstacles trying to stop us on the road to a better life. If we weather the storm by persevering, we will succeed and our new thoughts will become our new beliefs, and in turn, we will be able to manifest our desires and bring forth a different reality.

Mental Attitude

Our 'mental attitude' alone, can make the difference between our failure and success. We all face challenges, setbacks, fears, difficulties, mistakes, doubts, or obstacles over the course of our life. The way we react, or not, will determine the outcome we obtain. Some people let it break them, and others let it make them strong. Some will use it to learn and to grow while others will blame it for their failure or bad luck. Choosing to be positive, or to be negative, makes all the difference in the end. Sometimes, we feel negative and we think it is the only choice we have, but it is not so; we must decide to be in command of our mind and to adopt a positive mental attitude. Decide to put a stop to this 'mental beating'. Do not waste precious time to mull over negative experiences. Let go of negativity and be forgiving. When we fall, we get up, and not look back. Resolve to move forward with no regret, with no thought wasted on bad results or occurrences (remember, if you do, you are just putting in creative motion more of the same).

Some days we wake up feeling terrible, it seems like our world is falling apart. We cry and complain, and we want to stay in bed and sleep forever. We no longer want to struggle, feel pain, and / or keep living this way. This is a decisive moment, what we do at this precise point in time will determine if we are able to cross over to the other side, pass the test, overcome conditions, and experience a positive outcome. If we fall prey to our negative attitude, then we miss the opportunity to transcend that reality and bring forth transformation, change, manifesting, or reaching our goal. Often times, it is when we are really close to the finish line that our biggest challenge surface, to test our desire, resolve, and will. Remember, that having a positive mental attitude, at that particular moment, is the determining factor for our success.

If we are not yet able to fight the negative forces, i.e., if we succumb to our ego and negative inclination- then be forgiving and stop the self-beating. Do not compound the situation by indulging in the wrong mental attitude, by wasting time feeling guilty or bad about something that already happened; let the moment pass (and keep it in the past) and start anew. We need to tell ourselves, 'the next time I am going to do better and, I am better'. We need to move on and not let it hurt us even more. We must understand that a bad mental attitude is not doing us any good; it does not make us feel better and most importantly it keeps us away from reaching our goal. It only robs precious time, and prevents us from feeling and doing something good. Therefore, the next time we are facing something hard, we need to look inward, to our inner G_d- to muster the strength and to turn our back on that negative attitude and to choose the right attitude- to think and act positively. In practice, we need to think of and remind ourselves of the Eternal Truth of life. We need to fill our mind with G_d's love, abundance, peace, energy, power, etc... In moments of weakness, we can say to ourselves, 'G_d's love is within me and all around me, G_d is all good and is showering me with all that I need; abundance is mine. I am peaceful and Divinely guided in all that I do. I give thanks for G_d's help and direction. I fill my heart with G_d's love, energy, and peace.'

Further, we also need to keep in mind that to manifest our desire (health, success, wealth, etc...) does not call for any special talent or intelligence, **because the beauty of 'mind science' is that everyone is equal, we all have the same power and ability to co-create.** Our intelligence or talent is only a tool to help us choose or perfect, our goal. It enables us to be or to do- something that is compatible with our natural faculties and talents- in order to facilitate and to enjoy the process of manifesting. However, no matter what we choose, we must remember that we have the power and ability within us, to see all of our goals manifested. Give no attention to anyone that conveys an opposing idea. Give no thought to anyone that says that we need a certain talent or I.Q. to succeed. Recognize that the right mental attitude, along with our inner GPS, is all that we need to be able to manifest and to transform our life.

"Intuition is a very powerful thing, more powerful than intellect."

-Steve Jobs

Conclusion

While researching and writing this book I discovered so much more than what I had hoped for. Our mind, our soul, our life's purpose are all connected. Mind science teaches us the power of our mind. What we learn is that proper use of the mind can have miraculous effects on our life. When we use our mind the way the Creator intended we could have all that we desire. The reality we know is not all there is; our physical senses are not the only senses that are available to us. Our extra sensory senses and intuition are waiting to be uncovered. We must be open to grow spiritually in order to access the riches we all possess.

This book provides help to anyone seeking self-betterment and change. My greatest desire is to impart people with the knowledge and feeling that they can be and do anything they want.

The process of manifesting our desire is straightforward; for starters, there is no need for any prerequisites or any special skills. No one is more qualified than anyone else; we are all equals on the road to co-creating our reality. It is easy to grasp the concepts and ideas contained in this book. When we embark on our journey for change, the book guides us and provides all that we need to stay on course. We learn the necessary steps we must follow. The process is explained in detail without overwhelming us. It imparts within us the confidence and trust in what we are capable of doing or being. This book is our road map to manifesting a desired reality. We should read and refer to it as much as needed. It will always keep us connected and on track.

The human mind is such a treasure house, and it is our obligation to recognize the incredible gift that the Creator gave each one of us (without exception). All individuals have a mind with two distinct functions. One function is our intellect / ego. It draws its strength from our physical senses, the outside world, and the occurrences in our life (and all that they encompass). The other function of our mind is our intuition and inner knowing and power; it draws its force from the Creator, and the inner world within each one of us. The first one is our conscious mind, and the second one is our subconscious mind. The Creator also gave us the power of choice- free will- to decide which one we are going to listen to and follow.

In our daily life, we see this choice put to the test- when questions arise, when faced with challenges, when we are in need of advice, help, direction, or support- to whom do we turn? Do we look inward or outward? Are we using intellect alone, or are we looking deep into our subconscious mind? Do we panic? Are we afraid and worried? Are we connected to the Source of everything, or do we rely solely on ourselves for what we need? Do we believe we are in charge of our life, and we do not need help to solve or do anything? Do we ever entertain a thought for the Universe we live in, and for all of creation within it? Do we grasp the miracle that is our own human body? Do we listen to our gut and intuition? Do we turn to the Creator?

The truth is that when we turn to the Creator with questions, desires and needs, He answers us. When we ignore Him, and instead, we turn to people or ourselves, He, in turn, accepts our choice, and we are left to our own devices and physical capabilities to resolve any issue that comes up.

The beauty of life is the journey, and the growth that comes along with it. A life with no challenges or bumps along the way does not exist. If it did, then why would there be a need to choose anything (good over evil, or to be positive and not negative) since we would be content and not exposed to any negative situations. But in practice, the only way to test our choices and our faith, is to see how we interpret, react, or respond to seemingly bad or difficult happenstances. Thus, our response to pain, suffering, or chaos will determine how close or far we are from the Creator and the Eternal Truth of life. In practice, to confirm our faith that all is for our good; we need to live with confidence and the belief that everything the Creator makes is for the good; that there is no lack-supply of anything is infinite: love, peace, happiness, kindness, health, wealth, etc... That Divine standard is the norm we must follow in all of our endeavors. That when we turn inward, we can have all we need, and when we turn outward, we deal with the law of averages.

Most of us start out with a strong reliance on our conscious mind and intellect. The ego has a good hold on most of us. Our spiritual self has not yet awakened. However, when hardships or walls appear along the path, we are quickly made aware that the ego is of no great help. At first, we try to resolve the issues alone, by thinking that money, or people (like lawyers, doctors, bankers, etc...) are the solution. In reality, our issues would be solved more efficiently if we looked within for answers and guidance. But, we almost never think to look inward- to the Creator. As the Engineer-Maker and 'Manufacturer' of everything, the Creator is 'the One' best suited to solve any 'manufacturing' problems or issues. However, human nature is such that to want to be in charge is 'normal'. We arrogantly think we are the makers of the events in our life, and as such, the Creator lets us be in charge. He lets us try to figure it all out on our own. He does not interfere, since in fact, this is what we want. We are left unaided to solve the problems that arise. However, there (often) comes a time when a shift occurs and we are made to realize, through many of life's events, that the Creator is in fact needed and that we cannot do it all alone. The Creator is then there to love, guide, and help us, in all that we go through.

Mind science, and the road to manifesting a life that we want, is nothing more than recognizing the Creator and His relationship to us (through our subconscious mind). Once we grasp and appreciate the truth (that to create we need to connect), the rest are all small details and steps we need to follow in order to manifest. The starting point in mind science is to acknowledge the Creator, and his power of creation, to realize that we are all part of the Creator, and thus, we are all connected to Him (and to each other), and consequently, to His Infinite Power to create.

We are connected to Him through our soul and our subconscious mind- our creative mind. The

Creator is infinite, our souls are infinite, and our power to co-create is infinite. We are made in the image of the Creator, so in effect, our functioning mirrors His, but on a microcosm and individualistic level. Our inner G_d is nothing more than recognizing Him as the Creator, and our unity to Him, *via* our subconscious mind. Our inner power to manifest our desires comes from our subconscious mind, as the tool or medium that we use for our personal creation. Since G_d is everywhere at all times, He is within us at all times. 'Within us' means within our subconscious mind, and consequently, we can make use of this connection to co-create / to manifest what we desire.

The Creator wants us to enjoy all the good the Universe has to offer. He created us to live happy and fulfilled lives. He did not create us to be sick, depressed, homeless, alone, sad, afraid, lost, or unhappy. Love, peace, joy, abundance, health are not ideals or heavenly things, but to the contrary, are basic requirements everyone must have in this physical life. Lack is not the intended outcome; abundance and Infinite Supply is the reality. When we start to understand these concepts beyond mere theories, but rather, by applying them in practice in our everyday life- that is when we are truly ready and able to manifest anything. Our inner power works like magic, when our subconscious mind knows and feels what we desire and believes it as true; it connects to the Creator in order to co-create for us. Our will is the tool to maintain our focus on our desire, up until our desire is manifested. Thus, our inner solution is defined as persistent will, since nothing stands in the way of will.

The ultimate goal is to strive to be more, right now, and not to idealize the idea of some perfect self later. If we truly embrace and comprehend this, then we can live as role models, kinder people, which help others, and are not jealous of, or competing with anyone. In practice, this means that we incessantly make every effort to pursue peace, be loving, patient and compassionate, without hate, judgment, hostility, anger, or fear.

In order to stay positive and to be able to manifest, we need to regularly examine our beliefs, to make sure we are not harboring unwanted and destructive ones that hinder our progress. We must frequently question the motives that are behind our words or actions. Are they the result of thoughts of limited beliefs in lack or fear, or rather, do they reflect our faith and certainty in everything good? We need to make sure that the energy our thoughts and desires send out are positive. That the thought of our desire, stirs in us feelings of excitement and eagerness. At the root of our desire is the knowledge that we actually deserve to have it (i.e., Eternal Truth), and not because we hate our conditions and we are desperate (due to seeming lack or limitations).

No one is perfect, and we all need to work on ourselves. The goal is to work at it every day, overcoming faults and weaknesses, while always keeping in mind the long-term objective to be more.

However, when the ego is in charge, it gets in the way; it does not let us see the truth. When we over think we disconnect from Source Energy (since fear and anxiety are the cause), we thus, create confusion within our mind. When we do not learn to listen to intuition or to our gut feeling, then our intellect uses our physical world, environment, and conditions to process and grasp reality. This often leads to a negative state of mind that distorts concepts and ideas. Destructive thinking disrupts our ability to manifest and live our true destiny. In practice, what happens is that our intellect will find many reasons why we cannot do, have, or be. It delays our advancement.

Negative thinking goes against the essence of life and its tendencies, which are positive and lifeward. Life's movement-rhythm is growth, expansion, harmony, peace, love, health, abundance; it is all good-encompassing. Anything else, i.e., negativity, is in opposition to the purpose of creation, and does not allow for spiritual development. If we do not fully comprehend this point, we then miss seeing all the good we do have, and can have.

The 'thing' we have on top of our head, that we call the 'mind', is a 'marvel,' the depth of which we barely comprehend. Mind science gives us a small glimpse into its infinite capabilities, the scale of which human beings have not yet come close to understand, and thus, use. When we delve into our subconscious mind, we are touching the highest part of our being- our soul. The more we are connected to our soul, the more we are connected to our Creator, and the more we are connected to our individual creative power, our subconscious mind, and intuition.

This is our 'inner GPS', our personal tool to deal with any issue and to manifest our desires. We can count on it to give us the answers we seek as well as tell us what we have to do. It guides us and gets us to our desired destination.

As conscious beings with an intellect, we have choices: we have the choice to see things in a good eye, to speak words of truth, to act right or to think positively. When we train our conscious self to direct our thoughts and desires for a higher good, our life is so much better and fuller. Consequently, we are also imprinting our subconscious mind with these positive thoughts and beliefs. We are in fact elevating our personal frequency to the level of vibration needed to create a reality that reflects these positive thoughts.

Therefore, in reality, what we come to understand is that we do not need to make our primary goal the manifestation of something physical, since we are all able to manifest what we desire the moment we embrace life's Eternal Truth. Accordingly, what we need to do is to simply live by and apply that Truth. As such, when we are grateful and conscious of the Creator, then choosing happiness and positivity is not difficult.

Once we desire something that is in harmony with the Eternal Truth, our role is to only think of it, with faith (in the Creator and the outcome), by applying steady will, and letting go of the 'how and when'. Manifesting is actually a natural byproduct and a consequence of being all that we were meant to be- spiritual and higher beings- and not an end, in and of itself. Our thoughts create our reality, good or bad, so be careful upon which you place your focus and attention.

We need to understand that all the knowledge, lessons, and understanding in this book are just the beginning. It is now the time to take all that we have learned and to put it into practice. Theory without action leads to nothing. To live a higher life, a more spiritual life- one that is more responsible and more globally conscious- means that we adopt new positive ideas, new thoughts and beliefs, that in turn, become our new positive patterns of talk and action, which further in turn, become our new reality. Having faith in the process means to take the road less travelled, to face the unknown, and to know that hidden treasures await us. We are to strive for a life in which we continually learn, grow, and expand. If we do, then we are on the right path, the one that brings us to all the good we deserve.

The goal of this book is to help anyone seeking to achieve growth and betterment in his or her journey. It alleviates the process towards personal realization- to ultimately discover and trust our 'inner GPS' to guide, help, and manifest for us. This book is our companion, as well as a reminder, of all we are and have.

Bear in mind that the road to change and to excellence is never-ending, since we can always be more, do more, and give more. Our responsibility is to control our thoughts, prioritize, and stay positive. Keep learning, keep reading, keep doing everyday and you will remain connected and a co-creator. It is now the time to move forward and to live the life we were born to live.

I send you all best wishes and heaps of positive energy for fulfilling your dreams and manifesting the most meaningful life.

Resources

"Belief in limitation is the one and only thing that causes limitation."

-Judge Thomas Troward

Index

"Every great work, every big accomplishment, has been brought into manifestation through holding to the vision, and often just before the big achievement, comes apparent failure and discouragement."

-Florence Scovel Shinn

About the Author

Mathilde Benmoha Carro is a lawyer by profession with a passion for good manners and etiquette as well as for positive thinking and mind science. She holds a B.A., a law degree (LL.B), a master of laws (LL.M) and is a certified etiquette consultant. She has a website, 'goodmannersandetiquette.com' where she provides information on the subject. Her passion for everything mystical inspired her to learn the great works of many of the original thinkers in the field of mind science and metaphysics. She continues to research, study and share the knowledge she acquires, with the hope of helping as many people as possible. She lives in Montreal, Quebec.

"We tend to minimize the things we can do, the goals we can accomplish, and for some equally strange reason we think other people can accomplish things that we cannot. I want you to understand that that is not true. You have deep reservoirs of talent and ability within you that you can bring to the surface and achieve all that you desire."

-Earl Nightingale

Putting It into Practice

Mind Science Work Calendar

Exercise 1:   My Beliefs Are...

Exercise 2:   My Limited Beliefs Are...

Exercise 3:   My New Beliefs Are...

Exercise 4:   My Goals (Desires) Are...

Exercise 5:   My Affirmations Are...

Exercise 6:   I Am Grateful for...

Exercise 7:   I Forgive...and Let Go of...

Exercice 8:   I Ponder on Infinite Intelligence

Exercise 9:   My Daily Checklist

Putting It into Practice

"In visualizing, or making a mental picture, you are not endeavoring to change the laws of nature. You are fulfilling them."

–Genevieve Behrend

Mind Science Daily Calendar

Write down your daily schedule in order to keep the focus on your goal (insert times for: affirmations, visualizations, meditation, etc...).

Morning:
_____
_____
_____
_____

Afternoon:
_____
_____
_____
_____

Evening / Night:
_____
_____
_____
_____

_____

_____

_____

_____

_____

_____

_____

_____

_____

_____

_____

_____

_____

_____

_____

_____

_____

_____

_____

_____

_____

_____

_____

_____

_____

_____

_____

_____

_____

_____

_____

_____

_____

_____

_____

_____

_____

_____

_____

_____

_____

_____

My Beliefs Are...

My beliefs about (love, health, wealth, success, employment, fear, etc...) are... Write in detail what you feel and think about each belief.

_____

_____

_____

_____

_____

_____

_____

_____

_____

_____

_____

_____

_____

_____

_____

_____

_____

_____
_____
_____
_____
_____
_____
_____
_____
_____
_____
_____
_____
_____
_____
_____
_____
_____
_____
_____
_____
_____
_____
_____

_____

_____

_____

_____

_____

_____

_____

_____

_____

_____

_____

_____

_____

_____

_____

_____

_____

_____

_____

_____

_____

_____

_____

My Limited Beliefs Are...

Write what limited beliefs are blocking you and stopping you from realizing your dreams. (For e.g., fear, low self worth, not smart enough, not strong, not capable, unattractive, I am weak, not lovable, some people have more opportunities, I am not as good, I am bad, I am stupid, you need lots of money to start a business, you need a connection to get a great job, etc...)

_____

_____

_____

_____

_____

_____

_____

_____

_____

_____

_____

_____

_____

_____

_____

_____

_____

_____

_____

_____

_____

_____

_____

_____

_____

_____

_____

_____

_____

_____

_____

_____

_____

_____

My New Beliefs Are...

Write down your new beliefs that counter and replace your limited beliefs. (For e.g., I am smart, I can succeed, I can start my new business now, I am finding a good job, I can afford that new car, I am passing the exam with high marks, etc...)

_____

_____

_____

_____

_____

_____

_____

_____

_____

_____

_____

_____

_____

_____

_____

_____

_____

_____

_____

_____

_____

_____

_____

_____

_____

_____

_____

_____

_____

_____

_____

_____

_____

_____

_____

_____

My Goals (Desires) Are...

Write your goal in as much detail as possible (for e.g., if you want to start a business, write the type of business, the location, the amount of employees you have, the products/services you are selling, how much you plan to earn, who are your clients, etc... If your goal is to lose weight, set a precise amount of weight you want to lose and the time frame within which you are going to lose it (3lbs. / week, for e.g.). Give as much detail to your goal as possible.

_____

_____

_____

_____

_____

_____

_____

_____

_____

_____

_____

_____

My Goals (Desires) Are...

_____

_____

_____

_____

_____

_____

_____

_____

_____

_____

_____

_____

_____

_____

_____

_____

_____

_____

_____

_____

_____

_____

_____

_____

_____

_____

_____

_____

_____

_____

_____

_____

_____

_____

_____

_____

_____

_____

_____

_____

_____

_____

_____

_____

_____

_____

_____

My Affirmations Are...

Write a few positive affirmations about your new beliefs and goals and practice saying them a few times a day. (For e.g., 'I am a good employee and my boss appreciates and rewards my great work and contribution to the company. I am grateful to Infinite Intelligence for all the opportunities I get everyday to show my talent and expertise. I am well compensated and I enjoy very much what I do', or, 'G_d is healing me every day, and my body and all my organs are in perfect health. I feel good and energised. I give thanks to the Creator for my complete healing, I am good as new', or, 'Infinite Intelligence is showing me the path I must follow in order to achieve my goal, I am serene and peaceful, I know Divine intelligence will provide me with all the answers I need'. Or, 'I am well, I feel great', etc...)

_____

_____

_____

_____

_____

I Forgive... and Let Go of...

Insert names of people that you want to forgive and then write that you let go of negative emotions and feelings associated with them, such as, anger, resentment, blame, hostility, sadness, etc... (For e.g. 'I forgive John X for lying to me; I hold no resentment or ill feelings towards him. I wish him well.')

_____

_____

_____

_____

_____

_____

_____

_____

_____

_____

_____

_____

_____

I Ponder and Meditate on Infinite Intelligence

Who is my supply, what is my supply, why is supply infinite? Think about and write down examples of Infinite Supply in our life (grains of sand, fish in the sea, snowflakes, stars, rain drops, etc...) and be grateful for them and to the Creator.

_____

_____

_____

_____

_____

_____

_____

_____

_____

_____

_____

_____

_____

_____

_____

_____

_____

_____

_____

_____

_____

_____

_____

_____

_____

_____

_____

_____

_____

_____

_____

_____

_____

My Daily Checklist

At the end of every day put a check mark next to the activity you performed (try to make it a habit to do all the things on the list). It might seem like a lot, but it only takes a few minutes to put into practice.

⇒ I practice kindness

⇒ I focus on my goals

⇒ I avoid thinking of my conditions / environment and (current) unwanted reality

⇒ I make the effort to be positive and chase away negative thoughts by replacing them with positive thoughts

⇒ I think of the Creator and I stay connected to Him

Before Sleep:

⇒ I visualize one last time for the day; I never review the negative events / occurrences of the day

⇒ As I fall asleep, I think of beautiful images and positive thoughts, such as my goals / desires

"Busy your mind with the concepts of harmony, health, peace, and good will, and wonders will happen in your life."

-Dr. Joseph Murphy

"When the soul is starved for nourishment, it lets us know with feelings of emptiness, anxiety, or yearning."

-Menachem M. Schneerson

"If you won't be better tomorrow than you were today, then what do you need tomorrow for?"

–Nachman of Breslev

NOTES

NOTES

NOTES

www.ingramcontent.com/pod-product-compliance
Lightning Source LLC
Chambersburg PA
CBHW021154160426
42812CB00082B/2970/J